MYLES STANDISH,

WITH AN ACCOUNT OF THE

EXERCISES OF CONSECRATION

OF THE

MONUMENT GROUND ON CAPTAIN'S HILL,

DUXBURY, AUG. 17, 1871.

PREPARED BY STEPHEN M. ALLEN,
Corresponding Secretary of the Standish Monument Association.

BOSTON:
ALFRED MUDGE & SON, PRINTERS, 34 SCHOOL STREET.
1871.

KITCHEN OF THE STANDISH HOUSE.

MYLES STANDISH,

WITH AN ACCOUNT OF THE

EXERCISES OF CONSECRATION

OF THE

MONUMENT GROUND ON CAPTAIN'S HILL,

DUXBURY, AUG. 17, 1871.

PREPARED BY STEPHEN M. ALLEN,
Corresponding Secretary of the Standish Memorial Association.

BOSTON:
ALFRED MUDGE & SON, PRINTERS, 34 SCHOOL STREET.
1871.

CAPTAIN MYLES STANDISH.

THE character of the Pilgrims of New England probably stands out with more force and is as marked and distinctive as that of the pioneer settlers or conquerors of any country of which we read, while the result of their influence upon the nationality they created has been much wider spread, more various and beautiful, and giving life to a more liberal national and religious sentiment than that ever before engrafted in the hearts of any people. The Norman conquest, from which so much has been claimed for humanity, though so cruel and devastating in its first effects, and which for eight hundred years has exerted such an influence in the Old World, was conceived in sin, selfishness, and an unholy ambition, and was established with a vengeance diabolic and almost unheard of in the history of nations. The landing of the Pilgrims, and the settlement of Plymouth and Massachusetts Bay, on the contrary, gave birth to national ideas which were the offspring of a pure and supreme love of Deity, a free and untrammelled worship, and a government of universal liberty, based upon Christian principle, preceding, in all cases, the cravings for worldly gain or ambitious personal preferment. The sterling worth of a people in humble life, that would forsake home, friends, and country, cross the trackless ocean, and settle upon a frozen, barren shore, with privations and sufferings before them which they were certain to meet, shows the possession of a moral strength and force, that, perpetuated in their descendants, gives the New England people an ancestry of which they may justly be proud. Such were the founders of Plymouth in 1620, among whom there was one, a representative man, worthy in every respect to become a leader, who, without pretensions to special piety, worshipped acceptably at their shrine, guided their settlements, laid out their grounds, drew plans for their mills, collected and disbursed their money, sat for years at their council board, commanded their military forces, subdued their savage and bloodthirsty enemies, all without ever losing the confidence of the colony, or being doubted either as a Christian, citizen, soldier, or financier, and who died after long years of service, beloved and lamented to a degree seldom found in the conflicting associations of life.

Captain Myles Standish was born at Lancashire, England, probably in 1584. He descended from a long and illustrious line of ancestors of that name. Descending from Thurston de Standish and Ralph Standish, his family was divided and designated as the Standishes of Standish, and the Standishes of Duxbury Hall. They separated, — "Jordan" becoming the proprietor of Standish, and "Hugh" of Duxbury, one upholding the Catholic, the other the Protestant religion. The baronetcy of Standish, erected in 1676, became extinct in 1812. The family seats are situated near the village of Chorley, in Lancashire, and the property is large, the income being some five hundred thousand dollars per annum. The records of the parish from 1549 to 1652 were thoroughly searched a few years since by Mr. Bromley, the agent sent out by the heirs of Standish in this country, the result proving to his mind that Myles Standish was the true and rightful heir to the estates which were surreptitiously detained from him. Justin Winsor, in his History of Duxbury, says: "The records were all readily deciphered, with the exception of the years 1584 and 1585, the very dates, about which time Standish is suppesod to have been born; and the parchment leaf, which contained the registers of the births of these years was wholly illegible, and their appearance was such, that the conclusion was at once established, that it had been done purposely with pumice-stone, or otherwise, to destroy the legal evidence of the parentage of Standish, and his consequent title to the estates thereabout. The mutilation of these pages is supposed to have been accomplished, when, about twenty years before, similar inquiries were made by the family in America. The rector of the parish, when afterwards requested by the investigator to certify that the pages were gone, at once suspected his design of discovering the title to the property, and taking advantage of the rigor of the law (as he had entered as an antiquarian researcher merely), compelled him to pay the sum of about £15 or suffer imprisonment."

Miles was educated to the military profession, and early received a commission as lieutenant in Queen Elizabeth's forces on the Continent, in aid of the Dutch. He repaired to the Netherlands, the seat of war, where he remained a short time after peace was declared, but soon joined the English refugees of Leyden. He joined the first company of Pilgrims for America, and on their arrival on the coast was sent out in the command of the shallop with sixteen men, to make discoveries along the shore. After spending nearly a month in various expeditions, surveying the different bays and channels, he reported in favor of the harbor of Plymouth as a settling point, where the final landing was made. He was soon elected to the chief military command, a position he retained till his death, thirty-six years afterwards. There is, perhaps, no parallel of his military experience in the early settlement of the country.

"Standish affords us not only an instance of the nerve of the Pilgrims, but a type of their hearts." His courage was indisputable. In his various expeditions against the Indians he wanted but few men, and the choice of these he claimed for himself. He was always a leader in every hazardous undertaking, and the people, confiding in his bravery and prudence, were ever ready to place themselves under his command, and in the most trying conflicts they felt themselves secure. His actions show a forbearance rarely met with in one of his profession;

while in the time of decisive action, his courage and perseverance were equal to the boldest resolutions.

Winsor says: "In 1623 Standish was sent by the Governor, with orders to break up a plot of the Indians, which, it was learned, had been formed to destroy the settlement and massacre the inhabitants of the English colony at Wessagusset, now Weymouth. On this expedition, the most celebrated one of his life, and which is possibly a fair criterion of his character, he chose but eight men, refusing any more. On arriving at the settlement he found the people scattered, wholly unconscious of their impending danger. Having quickly assembled them, he informed them of their situation, not, however, without exciting the suspicions of the Indians. Soon after, an Indian bringing the Captain some furs, he treated him 'smoothly'; yet the Indian reported that he saw by the Captain's eye that he was angry in his heart. And at another time, Pecksuot, an Indian warrior of reputed courage, said to Hobomok, Standish's guide and interpreter, and an inmate of his household, that he understood that the Captain had come to kill him and the rest of the Indians there; but tell him, said he, we know it but fear him not — neither will we shun him, let him begin when he dares; he shall not take us unawares. And again, a little after, in the presence of Standish, whetting his knife before his face, and boasting of its quality, he said to him, 'Though you are a great Captain, yet you are but a little man; and though I be no sachem, yet I am a man of great strength and courage.' On the following day Pecksuot, Wittowamat, and his brother a youth of eighteen, and another Indian, with Standish and about the same number of his own men, being in a room together, the signal was given by the Captain, and the door instantly closed and fastened. Then seizing Pecksuot, he snatched his knife from his belt, and his men fell upon the others. A short struggle ensued, which ended in the death of Pecksuot by Standish, and that of the other Indians, save the youth, whom they afterwards hung. Hobomok, who stood by a silent spectator of all that passed, then smilingly exclaimed, 'Yesterday Pecksuot bragged of his own strength and stature, and told you that though you were a great Captain, yet you were a little man; but to-day I see you are big enough to lay him on the ground.'

"Consider the situation of Standish. Upon his decisive action at this moment we cannot but feel that depended much, — not merely the preservation of the company to whose succor he had come, but the existence, perhaps, of the whole colony. Had they been successful in their designs here, elated by their recent victory, they would have made the settlement of Plymouth the next object for their depredations, and the lives of the whole colony would have fallen victims to their cruel barbarity. His was not distant from the foresight of the captain. He struck a mighty blow, and, by determined action in a time of doubt, dispelled the fears of his followers and sent terror upon the enemy. This action needs no apology. He acted but the part of a brave defender of his country, who feels that upon his own vigorous exertions the defence of the people depends. And, says his biographer, men of his profession will admire his courage, his promptitude and decision in the execution of his orders."

No one has ever charged Standish either with failures in point of obedience, or of wantonly exceeding the limits of his commission. He is called by Prince one of those heroes of antiquity, "who chose to suffer affliction with the people of God; who, through faith, subdued kingdoms; wrought righteousness; obtained promises; stopped the mouths of lions; waxed valiant in fight, and turned to flight the armies of the aliens."

Near the close of his life, he was made commander of the expedition against the Dutch, and, although far advanced in years, he was still considered the best person upon whom the command could devolve. In his commission and instruction, he is spoken of as one "of whose approved fidelitie and abilitie we have had long experience."

Standish's services to the colony were of hardly less importance in their civil than in their military affairs. He held the office of an assistant and deputy during the whole of his life, was treasurer of the colony from 1644 to 1649, and once he was sent to England, as their agent. Scarcely an appraisement was made, where the colony were interested, but Standish was on the commission, unless otherwise occupied. About the year 1630, he settled in Duxbury, on a tract of land granted to him by the colony, and which has since been known as the Standish farm. Upon this farm the celebrated Captain's Hill is situated. Tradition fixes his house on the southeastern part of the peninsula, where there still remain the walls of two cellars, singularly joined at one end. It is supposed that the cellar of one part was constructed to accommodate a storehouse, built after his death, in 1656, by his son Alexander, which was supposed to have been burned some time during the next nine years, or previous to 1665. The present Standish house was erected by Alexander Standish, partly from old timbers taken from the remains of his father's house. This fact is fully verified by the appearance of the beams in the present building, which show not only the marks of former use, but bear traces upon them of the use of a whip-saw, an implement which antedated the establishment of saw-mills. It is also supposed that the hearthstone, as indicated in our engraving, belonged to the former house, as well as the doors and latchings, of which we also give a representation. There is nothing left to give the true size or shape of the original house, though the timbers that were transferred to the new one were mostly of oak, and were very strong. They are still quite sound, and show the old mortises and tenons used for the first house, in many places. The barn, so far as is known, was on the south slope of Captain's Hill, not far from the large rock, now sometimes called the "Captain's Chair." The homestead estate, containing about one hundred and fifty acres, was left, by will, to his son Alexander, who lived on it till his death, in 1702.

Alexander devised the homestead to his son Myles, who resided on it till his death in 1739. The latter left a numerous family. He also had a son Myles, who inherited the property, but who removed to Bridgewater, and died in 1784. The mother of the last named, and one sister, remained at the old home, and were probably the last of the family who resided there. The estate was sold by Myles, July 3, 1763, to Samuel and Sylvanus Drew, who disposed of the property to Wait Wadsworth, and from his hands it passed to George Faunce, and descended to his children; then a part was purchased of his grandson, George Faunce, and a part of Luther Pierce, by the present proprietor. The descendants of Captain Standish are very numerous, and are scattered through the whole country. Some remain in New England. Moses Standish, Lemuel Myles Standish, and one or two brothers reside in Boston, and William and Benjamin Standish, and perhaps some others, still reside in Duxbury and Plymouth County.

The Standish tract contains some of the finest land in the county of Plymouth, a part of which, on the east side, was the Elder Brewster place. Of Captain's Hill the historian of Duxbury says: "This hill formed a part of an early grant to Captain Standish, who settled near its base, and whose name it still bears. It is situated on a peninsula, which extends in a southeasterly direction, between the bays of Duxbury and Plymouth, and contains about two or three hundred acres of good soil, little inferior to any in the country in fertility."

"While in other portions of the town the soil is sandy and unproductive, and a considerable part in no state of cultivation, this peninsula is furnished with a deep and fertile soil. The same may be said of the highland on the Gurnet, Saquish, and many other similar spots around the bay, where the soil is in immediate proximity to the sea. Clark's Island in some parts possesses a mould, which, if equalled, is scarcely surpassed in the country; and while the northern and western sides offer the most desirable qualities for pasturage and grain, its southern and eastern declivities present a perfect garden, abounding with trees, through whose foliage, even during the summer's hottest months, stir the breezes from the sea. The summit of the hill is about four hundred yards from the sea, and about one hundred and eighty feet above its level, and when once attained, presents a view to him who communes with nature, and who has pondered over the history of the early Pilgrims, is acquainted with their character, and has conceived the purpose of their exile, — to him it presents a spectacle which has in times past, and which, I conceive, must ever cause an impression on his mind, not easily forgotten, and scarcely to be eradicated. Full as it is of the most pleasing associations, it calls up in the mind of the beholder those reminiscences which gladden his heart and arouse his soul into being, and clothe him with all the nobler feelings of mankind, dormant as they may lie within the deep recesses of his heart. Nor is the loveliness of the scene itself any the less an efficient agent of holy influences; both cause one to tremble, irresistibly, and to offer praise to his Maker. The circumstances, to be sure, add to the attractions of the spot; but its beauty, its simplicity of grandeur, its busy scenes, and its still, silent loneliness give to it a power whose effects need not be mentioned. Select, should you visit it, the closing hours of a summer's day, when the burning heat of the declining sun is dispelled by the cooler shades of approaching evening, and ascend to its height. Now as the retiring rays of day form on the heavens above a gorgeous canopy of variegated hues, so on nature's face below all brightens into richness, and the verdure of her covering softens into mildness; the shining villages around, and the village spires towering against a background of unfading green, add gladness to the scene. The glassy surface of the bay within, with its gentle ripplings on the shore beneath, the music of the dashing waves on the beach without, give quiet to the mind and peace within. Before you, in the distance at the east, appear the white sand-hills of Cape Cod, shining beyond the blue expanse, and seeming to encircle by its protecting barrier a spot dear to the heart of every descendant of that Pilgrim band. Still nearer, at your feet and before you, are the pleasant bays of Plymouth, Kingston, and Duxbury, enlivened by passing boats, and sheltered by the beach from a raging ocean, crowned at its southern extremity by a light-house, and with the extending arm of Saquish enclosing the Island of the Pilgrims; turning your eyes to the south, they fall in succession on the promontory of Manomet; on the ancient town of Plymouth, rising beneath, and as if under the protection of the mound beyond, the resting-place of the Pilgrim's dead, on the villages of Rocky Nook and of Kingston. Extending your eye over the extent of forest to the northwest, you see the Blue Hills of Milton, ascending far above the surrounding country; while nearer, at the north, are the villages of Duxbury and Marshfield, scattered over the fields, whose white cottages, shining in the sun, offer a pleasing contrast to the scene. Below you and around you once arose the humble abode of the Pilgrims. Who can gaze upon the spot which marks the site of the dwelling of Standish, without feelings of emotion? who can but give thanks that that spirit —

> 'A spirit fit to start into an empire
> And look the world to law' —

had been sent amongst them, to be their counsel in peace and their protection in danger? Who can but admire its ready adaptation to a sphere of action so totally different from the school of his youth? Here also arose the dwellings of Brewster, who having followed in his youth the retinue of kings and princes, preferred a solitary retreat in the western wilds, and there to worship his God in peace. Here, too, was the abode of Collier, who, under every circumstance of danger, strove with unceasing toil in the discharge of every duty necessary to the welfare and prosperity of the colony. Here, too, can be seen the spot whereon the habitation of Alden was, whose prudent counsels and whose rigid justice attained for him a rank in the estimation of the colony, alike an honor to himself, and a subject of pride to his descendants. Turn your vision as you may, and you will feel that you are gazing on a scene of more than ordinary interest, full of the most grateful recollections, and of a nature the most agreeable and pleasing."

"Scenes must be beautiful, which daily viewed
Please daily, and whose novelty survives
Long knowledge and the scrutiny of years, —
Praise justly due to those that I describe."

"Rose, the first wife of Myles Standish, died at Plymouth, January 29, 1621, about a month after the landing. She was among the first to succumb to the privations of that terrible first winter. He married a second wife (Barbara), who survived him.

"To his house on Captain's Hill, Standish removed after his second marriage, and here he drew around him a devoted class of friends, among whom were the elder Brewster, George Partridge, John Alden, Mr. Howland, Francis Eaton, Peter Brown-George Soule, Nicholas Byrom, Moses Simmons, and other set, tlers of Duxbury.

"The Indians also loved as well as feared him, and the faithful Hobomok ever kept near to minister to his wants, and was the faithful guide in his travels. This devoted Indian died in 1642, having faithfully served his master twenty years, and is supposed to have been buried on the south side of Captain's Hill, near the great rock called 'The Captain's Chair.' Tradition fixes his wigwam between two shell mounds on the shore near the Standish place, till taken home to the house of Standish, where he became an inmate till his death."

THE WILL OF MYLES STANDISH.

In the Plymouth Colony Records, vol. ii., pages 37, 38, is recorded the will of Standish, dated March 1, 1655. In this he devises that if he "die at Duxburrow, my body to be laid as near as conveniently may be to my two dear daughters, Lora Standish my daughter, and Mary Standish my daughter-in-law." After the payment of debts and funeral expenses he ordains that "my dear and loving wife Barbara Standish shall have the third part" of the estate.

4. I have given to my son Josiah Standish upon his marriage one young horse, five sheep and two heifers, which I must upon that contract of marriage make forty pounds, yet not knowing whether the estate will bear it at present; my will is that the residue remain in the whole state, and that every one of my four sons, viz., Alexander Standish, Myles Standish, Jerias Standish, and Charles Standish, may have forty pounds apiece; if not, that they may have proportionable to the remaining part, be it more or less.

5. My will is that my eldest son, Alexander, shall have a double share in land.

6. My will is that so long as they live single that the whole be in partnerships between them.

7. I do ordain and make my dearly beloved wife, Barbara Standish, Alexander Standish, Myles Standish, and Jerias Standish, joint executors of this my last will and testament.

8. I do by this my will make and appoint my loving friends, Mr. Timothy Hatherly and Captain James Cudworth, supervisors of this my last will, and that they will be pleased to do the office of Christian love, to be helpful to my poor wife and children by their Christian counsel and advice; and if any difference should arise, which I hope will not, my will is that my said supervisors shall determine the same, and that they see that my poor wife shall have as comfortable maintainance as my poor state will bear, the whole time of her life, which if you my

loving friends please to do, though neither they nor I shall be able to recompense, I do not doubt but the Lord will.

By me, Myles Standish, further my will is, that Mary Robinson, whom I tenderly love for her grandfather's sake, shall have three pounds in something to go forward for her two years after my decease, which my will is my overseers shall see performed.

Further, my will is that my servant, John Irish, Jr., have forty shillings more than his covenant, etc.

9. I give unto my son and heir apparent, Alexander Standish, all my lands, as heir apparent by lawful descent, in Ormstick, Borsconge, Wrightington, Maudsley, Newburrow, Crawston, and in the Isle of Man, and given to me as right heir by lawful descent, but surreptitiously detained from me, my great-grandfather being a second or younger brother from the house of Standish of Standish.

Myles Standish

The above described will, as indorsement states, was presented for probate by Captain James Cudworth, May 4, 1657. some time after the death of Captain Myles Standish.

Captain Standish is perhaps better known through Mr. Longfellow's charming poem relating to his courtship of Priscilla, than through the dry records of New England history, The historians of the Plymouth Colony have failed to give us the details of that remarkable wooing, leaving it to the poet to embalm the romantic story in his beautiful verse. We copy from the poem the following description of the doughty Captain: —

"In the Old Colony days, in Plymouth the land of the Pilgrims,
To and fro in a room of his simple and primitive dwelling,
Clad in doublet and hose, and boots of Cordovan leather,
Strode, with a martial air, Myles Standish the Puritan Captain.
Buried in thought he seemed, with his hands behind him, and pausing
Ever and anon to behold his glittering weapons of warfare,
Hanging in shining array along the walls of the chamber—
Cutlass and corselet of steel, and his trusty sword of Damascus,
Curved at the point and inscribed with its mystical Arabic sentence,
While underneath, in a corner, were fowling-piece, musket and matchlock.
Short of stature he was, but strongly built and athletic,
Broad in the shoulders, deep-chested, with muscles and sinews of iron;
Brown as a nut was his face, but his russet beard was already
Flaked with patches of snow, as hedges sometimes in November."

Captain Standish, in his old age, so far as can now be ascertained, enjoyed good health till his last illness. His vigor, both of mind and body, seemed as strong and fresh as in his early days. He combined in a pre-eminent degree the practical use of intuition and intellect; and when convinced of the wisdom of a plan, however suddenly made, he executed it with great rapidity. His temperament was sanguine and impulsive, but through the whole course of his life, he seemed to exercise a wonderful control over his passions.

He loved nature more than art, and entered with his whole soul into the enjoyments of his home and farm at Captain's Hill. His domestic and social life, and the great variety in the associations around this spot, seemed to captivate and control his very being. Here the careworn soldier found rest,—but rest only through that usefulness which ever brings happiness. Ever active and earnest, the full measure of his soul was drawn out in the many opportunities before him to serve his fellow-man, and the reward sank deep into a warm and tender heart, full of appreciation and love. The impetuous dreams of early life, the sense of wrong and injustice which drove him from the fatherland were here soothed and put to rest, and perhaps forever buried from thought in the consciousness of the emptiness of title, the possession of wealth, and the glitter of courts and palaces.

STANDISH MEMORIAL.

THE great interest taken by the public in the erection of some suitable memorial to Captain MYLES STANDISH, has properly taken the subject from the hands of a few of his immediate descendants, and placed it in charge of the American people at large, the representatives of whom, as shown by the list of the officers of the Association, are fully capable of taking care of the subject in all its bearings. The military of the United States very naturally claim a large share in perpetuating the memory of the first commissioned military officer of the New World, especially when the martial character of the man, after more than two hundred and fifty years' test, still stands out almost unparalleled in the history of the country.

It has often been said that the military powers of Standish, together with his great executive ability, and incessant labor in the various departments of the colony, saved it many times from dissolution. Be that as it may, there is abundant evidence that the colony always held him in high confidence and respect. The last commission against the Dutch, so near his death, proves that even in his old age their confidence was not diminished.

Members of the Grand Army of the Republic alone would cheerfully erect a monument; but some of our first merchants and citizens are too sensible of the great service of our soldiers to allow them to be at this expense, and offer liberally in its behalf. It is to be presumed that the sum of fifty thousand dollars can be easily raised for such a purpose. President Grant and many of his Generals have signified their hearty approval of the object, and citizens from almost every part of the country offer their aid and support.

The spot chosen for the monument is Captain's Hill, on the old Standish Farm, at Duxbury, where Captain Standish lived and died. This Farm was given him by the colony about 1630, and remained in the family till the middle of the last century. The hill is one hundred and eighty feet high, and overlooks Plymouth and Duxbury Bays, and is now much used as a sighting point to navigators in entering Massachusetts Bay. When the shaft is up it will be most useful to the coast survey as well as to navigators.

Thus, after two and a half centuries, this tribute is offered to the memory of one who left the allurements of wealth, luxury, and power, for the wilderness of New England, there to give a life service in sowing seeds for the fruit we to-day enjoy.

STANDISH MEMORIAL ASSOCIATION.

ARTICLE 1ST. The object and purpose of this Association is to cause to be erected a suitable and proper Memorial Monument, Obelisk, or Tablet, to the memory of Captain MYLES STANDISH, on or near Captain's Hill, Duxbury, Massachusetts.

ART. 2D. — The Board of Directors of the Association, for the time being, shall constitute the Board of Management, and have full power to act and do all things necessary to secure the object of the Association, appoint agents and assistants, and fill all vacancies in their board.

ART. 3D. — The property and funds of the Association may be held by one or more trustees, or a treasurer, who, with the officers of the Association, after the year eighteen hundred and seventy-one, shall be chosen by the subscribers to the fund, under such rules or by-laws as the directors or subscribers may adopt at any regular meeting.

ART. 4TH. — The officers of the Association shall be a President, one or more advisory or Vice-Presidents, Trustees and Directors, Secretaries and Treasurer, and such other officers or agents as may be appointed or chosen for the necessary purposes of the Association; and the Selectmen of Duxbury are to appoint or approve the first officers of the Association.

ART. 5TH. — The President, or any five Directors, may call a meeting of the Directors when needed. The annual meeting for the choice of officers and other business shall be held, after notice, the first Tuesday of January in each year. All officers may hold over till new ones are elected in their place.

ART. 6TH. — An Executive Committee of twelve shall be chosen, who shall have special charge of the planning and building the Monument, under the control of the Board of Directors.

ART. 7TH.— The foregoing Constitution, Rules, and Specifications may be altered and changed by the subscribers or directors at any regular meeting of the officers of the Association.

DUXBURY, December 21st, 1870, and the two hundred and fiftieth anniversary of the landing of MYLES STANDISH with the Pilgrims, at Plymouth, on the 21st day of December, 1620.

Officers of the Association appointed and approved by the Selectmen of Duxbury, July 4th, 1871.

PRESIDENT. — Gen. Horace Binney Sargent.

ADVISORY PRESIDENTS. — His Excellency Marshall Jewell, Connecticut; His Excellency James A. Weston, New Hampshire; Hon. Robert C. Winthrop, Massachusetts; Rev. Dr. George Putnam; Gen. Joshua L. Chamberlain, Maine; Hon. Alexander H. Rice; Dr. George B. Loring; Hon. John H. Clifford, Massachusetts; Gen. A. E. Burnside, Rhode Island; Hon. Nathaniel B. Shurtleff, Boston; Hon. E S. Tobey, Boston; Hon. Horatio Harris, Boston.

DIRECTORS. — Hon. Onslow Stearns, Concord, N. H.; Hon. Thomas Russell, Boston; Nathaniel Adams, Boston; Lemuel Myles Standish, Boston; Samuel Little, Boston; Samuel Loring,

Duxbury; Nathan Matthews, Boston; Frederick C. Adams, Kingston; Francis Standish, Boston; William Whiting, Boston; Nathan Morse, Boston; Isaac Keene, Duxbury; Jonathan S. Ford, Duxbury; Rev. Josiah Moore, Duxbury; Dr. James Wilde, Duxbury; James Ritchie, Boston; S. M. Allen, Boston; Edwin Adams, Boston; Edwin C. Bailey, Boston; Stephen N. Gifford, Duxbury; Joseph S. Beal, Kingston; Alden S. Bradford, Kingston; George B. Standish, Duxbury; Alden B. Weston, Duxbury; Elbridge Chandler, Duxbury; Hamilton E. Smith, Duxbury; Oliver Ditson, Boston; John G. Jackson, Boston; Dr. Cushing Webber, Boston; Gen. B. F. Butler; Jonas Fitch, Boston; Jacob H. Loud, Plymouth; George Bradford, Duxbury; John S. Loring, Duxbury; Harrison Loring, Boston; Joseph W. Coburn, Boston; Alden Frink, Boston; W. S. Danforth, Plymouth; George W. Wright, Duxbury; Dr. Calvin Pratt, Duxbury; Parker C. Richardson, Duxbury; Job A. Turner, Boston; Joshua M. Cushing, Duxbury.

SECRETARY. — Stephen N. Gifford, Duxbury.

CORRESPONDING SECRETARY. — Stephen M. Allen, Boston.

TREASURER. — Jacob H. Loud, Plymouth and Boston.

Committees chosen at the meeting at Duxbury, Aug. 17, 1871.

EXECUTIVE COMMITTEE. — Nathaniel Adams, of Boston; Lemuel Myles Standish, Hon. E. S. Tobey, Samuel Little, Francis Standish, James Ritchie, S. M. Allen, Edwin Adams, Jacob H. Loud, Harrison Loring, Job H. Turner, Gen. H. B. Sargent.

FINANCE COMMITTEE. — Horatio Harris, Hon. Alexander H. Rice, Hon. E. S. Tobey, Nathan Matthews, Oliver Ditson, Dr. Geo. B. Loring, Samuel Little, Jacob H. Loud, Nathaniel Adams, Jonathan S. Ford, George B. Standish, Gen. B. F. Butler, George W. Wright, Jonas Fitch, W. S. Danforth, Hon. Nathaniel B. Shurtleff, Rev. Dr. George Putnam, and Joseph S. Beal.

EXERCISES OF CONSECRATION ON CAPTAIN'S HILL

DUXBURY, AUGUST 17, 1871.

THE first train on the new Duxbury and Cohasset Railroad arrived at the Duxbury station at seven o'clock the evening previous, with freight and passengers, and bringing a section of two guns and twenty men of the First Battery, under command of Capt. E. C. Langley and Lieut. I. C. Foster. On the morning of the seventeenth, on the arrival of the cars and steamboat, the exercises of the day commenced with the firing of one hundred guns by the batttery.

A procession was formed at the depot, under the direction of Joshua M. Cushing, the marshal of the day, the Standish Guards, Lieut. Lanman, commanding, acting as escort.

Arriving at the monument grounds, the assembly were called to order by Gen. SARGENT, President of the Association, and the Executive and Finance Committees were appointed, and the exercises progressed as follows:—

MUSIC BY THE WEYMOUTH BAND.

Hail to the Chief.

PRAYER.

BY REV. JOSIAH MOORE.

ODE TO MYLES STANDISH.

AIR — *America.*

Sung by the Audience.

ALL Hail, departed Chief!
The Nation to thee brings
An offering free;

Not of mere bronze or stone,
Nor set on hill alone, —
Our memories long have flown
O'er land and sea.

Fond hopes in Britain left,
Of wealth and power bereft,
Still, spirit free,
You braved the ocean's roar,
You wooed a frozen shore,
That we might evermore
Wed liberty.

That seed of freedom sown,
Through frost and blood hath grown
A Nation free!
An empire, great in trust,
A people full of rest,
Millions, thus happy blest,
All honor thee.

After the singing, General Sargent was formally introduced to the audience, by the Secretary, Mr. Gifford, and addressed them as follows: —

ORATION.

BY GEN. HORACE BINNEY SARGENT.

It would have been more fitting to the grandeur of a noble memory that a distinguished connection of Myles Standish should have addressed you to-day. It would have been most agreeable to myself, as well as to you, that one of the many, illustrious by letters or by deeds, with whom the Pilgrim blood is blessed, should enjoy the honor of speaking before an audience familiar with the simple, grand traditions which I can only repeat like a twice-told tale to you. I crave your courteous patience for my short recital of a well-known story, and my reverent tribute to a life supremely brave.

Two memorable pictures, representing widely separate decades, hang on the wall of American history. Two and a half centuries span the gulf of time between the first decade, when a little band of Englishmen floated into Jamestown, and another little band, a few years later, became entangled in the shoals of Cape Cod; and the last decade, when, with a shock of arms that shook the world, the descendants of the Cavaliers, repeating English history, surrendered the wreck of all their armies, — infantry, cavalry, and cannon, — with all hope of separate empire, to tne descendants of the Puritans and to national supremacy; each combatant bound to the other, henceforth forever, by mutual reverence for proven valor; both, victor and vanquished, destined to stand hereafter, shoulder to shoulder, against the world in arms, and clasp each other's hands as brethren, — joint heirs of all America!

The giant timbers of English oak with which Nelson humbled France would once have been an easy prey to the tiniest squirrel of the wood. And the germ acorn did not more differ from the line-of-battle ship, than did the colony of the Mayflower from our veteran nation of to-day. As the oak had gathered to itself all elements of the universe from ten thousand storms and showers, until its top reached out to heaven, and its roots, like anchors, grappled with the world, so the colonies have incorporated the energies and assimilated the qualities of many peoples. But the germ principle has controlled them all. As no method of culture, no fertilizing agent, no icy cold or fiery heat, would have developed the acorn into anything but the oak, so the Pilgrim spirit, while absorbing, with all the vigor of vitality, the masses of life, wealth, poverty, ignorance, and culture that have been wafted to these shores, could grow into nothing else than an independent, popular government. Dissenters from those who dissented — even from dissent — must necessarily have founded a state with an inborn, hereditary tendency to rebel against assertion of creed or sceptre. The fugitive residents of the home-like community of Leyden, which, after an exhausting war, had chosen the princely boon of a university rather than immunity from onerous taxation, might naturally develop that cradle of independent thought, — the common school-house.

But to develop anything, it was first of all essential that the Pilgrim colony, stranded on a sterile cape in a New-England winter, among savages, should survive. And the wonderful providence of God is not more evident in the protecting husk that he gives to the ungerminated acorn, with which, amid the thunder of battle, he purposes to override a nation, than it is in creating the Moses and the Joshua to lead an infant people. The rough tent of a trooper, the unsurveyed forests of Virginia, the flat-boat of the Mississippi, the rude log-cabin of the West, as well as the sheep-folds of Israel or the cattle-shed of Galilee, may contain the fate of empires.

About the time that all Christendom was in mourning for the murdered Prince of Orange, and deploring in his death the overthrow of the bulwark of the Protestant faith, a little fair-haired child was playing among the hedge-rows of England, who was destined to learn the art of war in the armies of that king's more warlike son, Prince Maurice, then a boy of seventeen, and to be a tower of defence to the unsoldierly Pilgrim colony of Protestant America.

That child — whose bones, after nearly fourscore years of toil and war, were laid somewhere on this hill-side, perhaps under our unconscious feet — was Myles Standish, the great Puritan captain! He was born about the year 1580, of English ancestry, dating back to rank and opulence as far as the thirteenth century. Of his childhood, little is known. To defeat the title of his line to lands in England, the rent-roll of which is half a million per annum, the hand of fraud is supposed to have defaced the page that contained the parish record of his birth. Unjustly deprived of these vast estates, as he avers in his will, in which he bequeaths his title to his eldest son, it seems probable that he went to Holland near the time of his majority. Queen Elizabeth signed his commission as lieutenant in the English forces, serving in the Netherlands against the cruel armies of the Inquisition. As she died in 1603, about two years after his majority, it is not improbable that we are indebted to that first disappointment, which may have driven him, in his early manhood and some despair, into the army.

From 1600 to 1609, the year of the great truce between Prince Maurice and the King of Spain, the contest was peculiarly obstinate and bloody. In this fierce school the Puritan captain learned the temper and art of war.

From 1609 to 1620, a period of truce but not of civil tranquillity, the Low Countries were inflamed by those theological disputes of the Calvinists and Arminians which brought the excellent Barneveldt to the scaffold, and drove the great Grotius — a fugitive from prison — into exile. In this school, perhaps, Myles Standish learned some uncompromising religious opinions, which brought him into strange sympathy and connection with the Pilgrim church in Leyden. Both periods seemed to leave their impress on his character. The inventory, recorded with his will, mentions the Commentaries of Cæsar, Bariffe's Artillery, three old Bibles, and three muskets, with the harness of the time, complete. His Bibles were old. A well-worn Bible for every musket; and, thank God, a musket, not an old one, to defend each Bible!

The schedule of his books, some forty in number, records nearly twenty which are devotional or religious. With the memory of one act of singularly resolute daring, when, in obedience to the colonial orders to crush a great Indian conspiracy, he took a squad of eight picked men into the forests, and deemed it prudent to kill the most turbulent warrior with his own hands, we may imagine how the pilgrim soldier, friend and associate of Brewster, disciple of the saintly Robinson, rose from the perusal of one of the old Bibles, or of "Ball on Faith," "Sparkes against Heresie," or "Dodd on the Lord's Supper," to stab Pecksuot to the heart with his own knife; a giant who had taunted him with his small stature in almost the very words of Goliah, in his insulting sneer at David, long before; and to cut off the head of Watawamat, which bloody trophy the elders had ordered him to bring home with him. We can imagine him on the evening of that cheaply victorious day, taking more than usual pleasure in the exultant psalms of the warrior David, and in a chapter of Burroughs's "Christian Contentement" and "Gospell Conversation," especially as he had his three muskets with bandoleers, and Bariffe's Artillery, close at his hand. One can feel the unction with which the valorous pilgrim would religiously fulfil the colonial order to smite the heathen hip and thigh, and hew Agag in pieces before the Lord.

Not originally, and perhaps never, a member of the Pilgrim church, and possessing many traits which might have belonged to the fierce trooper, in an army whose cavalry was the legitimate descendant of Cæsar's most formidable enemies, — the Batavi, celebrated for cavalry qualities, and long the body-guard of the Roman emperors, — the appearance of the somewhat violent soldier, in the saintly company of Parson Robinson's church, is an anomaly.

It has been proven many a time, from the days of Bannockburn, when the Scottish host sank on its knees to receive the benediction of the Black Abbot of Inchaffray, even to our own late day, when many of the best fighting regiments were blessed with the most earnest chaplains, that men never tender their lives more gallantly to God and mother-land than when they are fervently preached to and prayed for.

Yet the all-daring contempt for peril, the roughness of temper, the masterly economy with which Standish saved human life by consummate indifference to personal homicide upon prudent occasion, his power of breathing his own fiery heart into a handful of followers, till he made them an army able to withstand a host in the narrow gates of death, would lead us to expect such a colleague for the saintly Brewster as little as we should expect to see Sheridan —

> "Cavalry Sheridan,
> Him of the horses and sabres we sing" —

prominent among the Methodists.

In truth, with the poem of our sweetest and most cultured bard in our minds, and with the memory of those fierce monosyllables with which our great cavalry leader rolled back defeat upon the jubilant rebel host, and rescued victory at Winchester, fancy can depict the foaming black horse pressed into the rush of the shell-shattered guidons by the iron gripe of knees booted in "Cordovan leather," and imagine that little Myles Standish rode that day in the saddle of little Phil Sheridan.

To the genealogist, who believes that names represent qualities and things, it is not unpleasing to find in the family record of Standish and Duxbury Hall, in the parish church of Chorley, Old England, the name Milo Standanaught. To stand at nothing, in the way of a duty commanded by the civil authority, seemed the essence of character in Myles Standish; and thoroughness stamps the reputation of the name and blood to-day.

The materials for personal biography are scanty. His wife, Rose Standish, — an English rose, — whose very name augurs unfitness for a New-England winter on an unsettled cape, died within a month of the landing. A light tradition exists that his second wife, Barbara, was her sister, whom he left an orphan child in England, and sent for. She arrived a woman grown, and the valorous captain added another illustration to the poet's story, that Venus and the forger of thunderbolts were married.

From the first anchorage, Captain Standish, as the soldier of the company, was charged with all deeds of adventure. At first, certain grave elders were sent with him for counsel. But ultimately his repute in affairs, both civil and military, was such that he was for many years the treasurer of the colony, and, during a period of difficulty, their agent in England. As a soldier, he was evidently the Von Moltke of the Pilgrims. They invested him with the general command. Even in extreme old age — the very year that he died "very auncient and full of dolorous paines" — he received his last and fullest commission against new enemies, his old friends, the Dutch.

It is singular that among the primitive people, who must often in the later Indian wars have missed his counsel and conduct, as the poet describing Venice, sighs, —

> "Oh! for one hour of blind old Dandole,"

no clear tradition has descended of the place where the war-worn bones of the soldier-pilgrim lie. Sent, like Moses, to guide and guard a feeble people to a promised land of power that he might never see, no man knoweth his burial-place until this day.

More than one hundred years ago, the following paragraph appeared in the Boston "News-Letter," dated Boston, January 22, 1770: "We hear from Plymouth that the 22d day of December last was there observed by a number of gentlemen, by the name of the Old Colony Club, in commemoration of the landing of their ancestors in that place."

The fourth toast on that occasion, a hundred and one years ago, was, "To the memory of that brave man and good officer, Capt. Miles Standish."

Over the graves of the guests at that dinner, —

> "For fifty years the grasses have been growing."

But the principle of public fidelity shares the immortality of God and Truth. Reverence for it never dies till the decay of nations. And to-day we come together, the dwellers in the city and the dwellers on the shore, men of every age and all professions, to dedicate one spot of this parental soil for an enduring monument to the same Myles Standish of the same unfaded record. The sunlight of near three hundred years, that has shone fatally on many a reputation since his baby eyes first saw the light of England, has only brought out the lasting colors of his fame.

Believing, as I firmly do, that he was a useful, a necessary citizen, because he was "that brave man and good officer" at a time when soldierly qualities were essential to the very life of the infant colony, it seems to me providential for the colonists that one of their number was, by temper and training, unable to sympathize with that soft tenderness for human life which is wont to characterize saintly-minded men, like the Rev. Mr. Robinson, who, when he heard of the marvellous conflict where Standish, with three or four others, in a locked room, killed the same number of hostile chiefs that were gathering their tribes to exterminate the English, uttered these sorrowful words: "Oh! that you had converted some before you had killed any!" The soldier practised that terrible piece of economy which no saint of the company would have dreamed of doing with his own hand. To borrow the diction of the time, the gauntlet of the man of wrath was the fold of the lambs of God. It was fortunate for us who believe in Plymouth Rock, that one trained soldier, who had faced war conducted by the Duke of Alva, came out in the Mayflower. Some little love of high position, some thirst for gain in office, some disposition to confer office on men for their "forwardness" rather than for their fitness, were seeds of weeds that the Mayflower brought over to the congenial soil of America. Even in the second expedition inland from the barque, "the Gunner was sick unto death," "but hope of trucking made him go." It is to be feared that the mantle of that gunner falls upon some camp-follower in every regiment.

Had the fate of the Pilgrims depended on such motives, Elder Brewster and his company would have been buried in some Krossaness, like the earlier explorer, the son of Eric the Red, and American civilization might have been for centuries deferred.

Myles Standish represented the true idea of public service, vigorous fidelity and trained fitness for his place. In his single heroic person he exhibited the true idea of the army, — skilled military force in loyal subordination to the civil authority. The confidence that the colony reposed in him to execute their most difficult commands as a citizen soldier, seems to prove that he revered, in the words of Mr. Robinson's farewell sermon, "the image of the Lord's power and authority which the magistrate beareth," — words that can never be too forcibly impressed on the minds of the penny-wise, who would diminish the dignity of the magistrate's office by inadequate compensation, or destroy his independence by the vulgar device of the social charlatan, gifts to supplement judicial salaries. If one may venture on such high speculation, it may be that God is just, partly because he is supreme, and to Him belongs the earth "and the fulness thereof." Freedom from obligation is of the essence of independence in the magistrate who bears "the Lord's power and authority."

As a dissenter from dissenters, saturated with the spirit of liberty, Standish, as an agent of authority, never fell into the heresy with which the rogues of the body politic cajole its fools,—that a weak execution of the laws, an imbecile or impotent manifestation of government, is test or evidence of freedom. Nor did the Northern Pilgrims ever fancy that a government founded upon compact was less panoplied with positive authority, within its sphere, than the superior government of the crown.

Even when every English life was precious to the settlements, the Pilgrims did not hesitate to execute three Englishmen for the murder of one Indian. In flying from civilization to a desert in pursuit of liberty, the Pilgrims did not fly so fast and far as to leave majestic law behind them. That dear, pale banner of the State, which the great-hearted, true-hearted, stout-hearted war minister of Massachusetts, John Albion Andrew, of all-blessed memory, thanked God that no one of fifty-three regiments then in commission had ever left on any field of battle, bears the device that might have been inspired at that early hour,—an Indian erect, in all the dignity of manhood, ready for peace or war, and the armed hand of protecting power raised above him, ready to guard or smite, and the legend *Ense petit placidam sub libertate quietem.*

And this is the end and path of government,—the armed hand, seeking serene repose, under liberty, by the sword, raised, but not needlessly descending; or if kept in the scabbard, kept always sharp.

To us, who sometimes ignore the uncancelled, unpaid debt of the nation to the military academy, and to the professional soldiers who there learned the art of victory; — to us, who sometimes imagine that the practice of gymnastics, with a musket, makes all the difference between a citizen and a citizen soldier, and dispenses with that code of new sensations, subordination, the soldierly habit of mind and temper, exact obedience and reverent loyalty to authority, which no muster-field or training-day can give, and which nothing but military discipline in a camp of instruction can inspire; — to us, who have learned, by bitter experience, how much time and blood and gold it costs to convert a patriotic mob into an effective army of soldier citizens; — to us, who are suffering oppressive taxation for our ignorance and forgetfulness that true economy is always to be prepared for war, a blunder and a crime which we have no moral right to fasten upon the purses of posterity, for the blunder was our own; — to us, thus criminal and suffering, it is profitable to reflect, that if Myles Standish had not been a trained soldier, the reverend heirs of the elders of the little church of Leyden would probably have adorned the wigwams of "the Massachusitts." His grand heart might have been as true and loyal and brave as it was; his arm — now dust, mouldering somewhere under the sod of this hill-side — might have been as strong. But if he had not learned from his own experience, and the well-conned commentaries of his beloved Cæsar, how contemptible are the most vigorous and patriotic multitudes without real discipline, Plymouth Rock would have been of no importance except to some leisurely antiquarian; Northern civilization would have been smitten with sudden death by savage tribes; even this beautiful headland might have been tilled by Virginian slaves to-day.

Special fitness for special work — education adapted to a purpose — is the lesson taught by the Pilgrim life. Well might we profit by it, in teaching the industrial arts of common life to the pupils of our common schools, which now, neglecting the practical arts of daily household duties, fill the world with helpless people, — starving, lady-like teachers, without pupils; accountants, who have nothing to add up, — useless members of society, ignorant of every duty that a home demands, and demanding a home that their refinement craves and station cannot give. That even the Pilgrims found, that overmuch unpractical culture was incompatible with provision for the needs of rugged life, is indicated by the fact that the second generation was less refined and more skilled in practical arts than the first.

To be the founders of states is the first of glories, according to Lord Bacon. The career of our Pilgrim hero is a beautiful illustration of an education fitted to the great mission for which he seemed peculiarly, strangely ordained.

In grateful memory we consecrate this spot of earth to a monument of the great Puritan captain. May its shadow fall upon his grave! For two centuries the stars have looked upon it. At what moment of the night the circling moon may point it out with shadowy finger, no mortal knows. No mortal ear can hear the secret whispered to the night, "Beneath this spot lies all of a hero that could die."

High as the shaft may tower over headland and bay, deep as its foundation-stones may rest, brightly as it may gleam in the rising or setting sun upon the mariner returning in the very furrow that the keel of the Mayflower made, the principles of common-sense, a citizen soldier's education for a citizen soldier's work, the principles of moral truth, manly honesty, prudent energy, fidelity incorruptible, courage undauntable, all the qualities of manhood that compel unflinching execution of the states' behest, — are firmer and higher and brighter still. And to crown them all is reverence to the Supreme Executive of Earth and Heaven, who knows no feebleness of heart or hand, and whose great purpose moved the war-worn Pilgrim's feet to seek his home upon this rock-bound continent, where the unceasing waves of two unfettered oceans roar the choral hymn of Freedom.

General Sargent's address was listened to with marked attention and received frequent applause as he alluded in glowing terms to the heroic virtues of the founder of the town of Duxbury.

MUSIC BY THE BAND.

CONSECRATORY PRAYER.

BY REV. R. H. NEALE, D. D

HYMN. — OUR PILGRIM FATHERS.

AIR — *Auld Lang Syne.*

Sung by the audience.

AWAKE! the slumbering Hero comes!
  Arise! his spirit nears,
To marshal back to "Pilgrim Homes"
  Our sires from other spheres.
For "Auld Lang Syne" they come,
    For "Auld Lang Syne,"
And gather round those "Pilgrim Homes,"
    Of "Auld Lang Syne."

Hosannas to our Pilgrim Sires!
  Bright memories round them twine;
Our prayers invoke celestial lyres
  Around their homes divine.
For "Auld Lang Syne" we sing,
    For "Auld Lang Syne,"
All honor to our Pilgrim Sires,
    For "Auld Lang Syne."

At the close of the exercises on the monument grounds, a procession was formed for the dinner tent, which was reached at about half-past two. Gen. Sargent led the guests, consisting of General Butler, General Schouler, Dr. Geo. B. Loring, Hon. Jacob H. Loud, Hon. Josiah Quincy, Ex-Mayor Shurtleff, Mayor Gaston, Hon. William T. Davis of Plymouth, members of the Executive Council, and Hon. Oliver Warner, Secretary of State, Rev. Dr. Caswell, Hon. A. C. Barstow, Rev. A. A. Miner, Rev. Edward E. Hale, Hon. Otis Cary, and others.

After the company were seated, they were called to order by General Sargent. Prayer was offered by Rev. Dr. Burgess. After about an hour spent in eating, General Sargent rapped to order, and introduced the speech-making by expressing the satisfaction which he enjoyed, after having been tortured by making a speech earlier in the day, to torture other gentlemen by calling upon them for speeches. In introducing the first toast, he made very complimentary allusion to Gen. Butler, which was applauded.

He announced the first regular toast as follows: "The President of the United States, and the great Puritan Captain: trained soldiers both, and none the less determined to carry out the will of the people without any policy of their own."

Responded to by General Butler.

SPEECH OF GENERAL BUTLER.

Mr. Chairman, Ladies and Gentlemen: —

I grieve that the principal executive officer of the United States in this Commonwealth, who came with me here, and who would in the usual course be called upon to respond to the toast to the president of the United States, has been called back by imperative necessity, and left that which he, as a son of Plymouth, would be glad to perform, to be performed by me.

As I ascended Captain's Hill this morning, the thought occurred to me how little each generation knows of the effect of the events which occur in its own time. How little our pilgrim fathers thought of the great country which thereafterward their ideas and their descendants were to govern; when the little Mayflower entered this bay, how little thought those pilgrims of the great work they were doing! So each and every great event; to the present — to the accompanying generation, the work is a small one, however great it may seem to those who come after. The great Captain, dead as we are told by your orator and by tradition, has an unknown grave. We can hardly look back and believe that the man that we know, the great citizen soldier of iron will, of that Pilgrim band, would be so little remembered by those that immediately surrounded and came after him, that his resting-place should be even a matter of which tradition does not speak. He has but suffered the fate which all events of great magnitude, rising from small beginnings, suffer at the hands of their contemporaries.

After what has been said — nay, after what the men of Plymouth know of Myles Standish — it would be idle for me, coming from Essex County, to enter into anything like eulogy. He came down, indeed, once to Essex County, however, and it was the only time when he went out and came not back victor. But then he interfered with our fish! (A laugh.) There is a trait developed in the Puritan pilgrim character in the steady public employment of Myles Standish, which deserves a moment's thought. No more pious, nay, no more thoroughly religious people, ever came together. They came here, not as tradition has it, not in the words of poetry, for the purpose of establishing freedom to worship God, but they came here for the purpose of establishing a commonwealth in which they should have the right to worship God uninterfered with by any other class, or power, or potentate whatever; and upon that theory alone can we, their descendants, entirely justify every act of theirs. If they simply meant to establish freedom to worship God, why did Roger Williams found Rhode Island? Why did they cast out the schismatic? It was because they thoroughly believed they were right; that their religion was the true religion. They, believing that, had left the perfect freedom ot Holland, where they had every religious freedom except the freedom of worshipping undisturbed by schisms and dissensions, and came here to this country. And when they made themselves a home in the wilderness, they determined that, being right, having made the great sacrifices for that right which they had done, no man should interfere with them. They carried out their own ideas to the logical consequence; better that men should suffer in this world, than to suffer an eternity in the next, as they believed all men who substantially differed from them would. They always stood by the logic of their own ideas. And it is the standing by that logic that to-day gives those ideas the government of the nation, and makes this nation the missionary nation of religious freedom and religious rights in the world.

Again, our Pilgrim fathers were practical men. Deeply imbued with the religious spirit, believing they were controlled by a Divine Providence, they recognized the fact that that Providence worked through means, and human means, and used all human means best adapted to carry out the end. They remembered that Providence always blest the best battalion and the best soldiers. They believed in the man who had a will, and they believed that their prayers would be sufficient to enable him to carry out the will and power of God, although the man might not be the most proper instrument in a religious point of view.

One of the most marked characteristics of Myles Standish was, that, living among the Puritans, among religious men, not a hypocrite, not praying in public and sinning in private, and willing his whole life should be known and well understood, he carried with him, from the beginning to the end, the uttermost confidence and respect of the highest religious people. True, the good Elder Robinson thought that he might convert a few of the savages before he slew them, but he was quite content that the Indian might be slain provided that God's people might be preserved. Myles Standish had a will of his own, and he chose to exercise that will, and whenever it became necessary for him to carry forward the work he had in hand, to do the duty placed upon him, he was ready to sacrifice any enemy of his country which stood between him and the work which he was delegated by his country to perform.

Again, Myles Standish had another high attribute of character, and that was loyalty to law — loyalty to authority. He never went beyond the right as it was given to him; he always bowed to the civil power, and in that he only showed his training as a soldier. This idea General Butler elaborated, and claimed that the same thing was shown in the late civil war, when our soldiers showed themselves obedient always to law and order, especially on their return home, when they were expected to make trouble. He paused to eulogize General Grant, in this connection, whom he termed the second great soldier of this country since Myles Standish. The latter had thirty-six years of executive power, and there are those who hope General Grant may continue many more years to execute the will of the nation. (Applause.) Whatever else was said about General Grant, they could not claim that his policy had been against the will of the people.

There was a resemblance between Myles Standish and General Grant in the way they have been treated by their countrymen. Some persons objected that a grateful people should make gifts to General Grant, but did not our Pilgrim fathers give the land on which they then stood to Myles Standish for his soldier's duty done? *Thank God, in those days there were not any newspapers,* and there was no slander raised on that account. (Laughter.) In this regard, General Butler thought the example of the Pilgrim fathers might well be followed. Here was sown the seed which enabled this country to go through the war for the suppression of the Rebellion. He (Butler) was one of those who believed that the Rebellion was necessary, and that it could not be averted; that all in the country were more or less guilty of the great cause — African slavery; that the war was sent for the nation's regeneration. He remembered that Massachusetts and Rhode Island once owned slaves, and although subsequently rid of them, the North was guilty of participation in the slavery of the South. He believed the war could never have ended until emancipation was proclaimed and the nation cleansed by fire. Any man, looking back over the recent events, could, in his opinion, see the guiding hand of Providence in them all. As Moses was not allowed to set foot on the promised land, so President Lincoln was not allowed to enter into the full enjoyment of being the ruler of a reunited people, and the nation had to have the last of all phials of wrath in the shape of his successor. The triumph of the Puritan over the Cavalier was referred to, and General Butler said so strong a faith had he in the Puritan character that he was almost superstitious about names, even, and if his grandfather's name had been Carlos instead of Zephaniah, he did nt' believe he would have gone to the late war. It is this Puritan idea that is revolutionizing the whole country to-day; and when in the South and elsewhere shall be established schools, equal rights, the town house, the church where the word of God shall be preached to satisfy the dictates of the consciences of those who desire to hear it, the nation will be redeemed. He (General Butler) observed some persons smiling at his last remark, and repeated it, and declared that it was the Puritan idea not to impose their tenets on anybody else, and to allow nobody to impose their tenets upon them. In closing, General Butler alluded to the Christian commission following our armies in the late war, and claimed that it was a strictly Puritan institution, and ended with the following sentiment:

"The Puritan idea, the motive power which is to revolutionize the world."

After music by the band, the second regular toast was given "to the Commonwealth of Massachusetts," and both Gov. Claflin and Lieut.-Gov. Tucker being absent, Hon. Oliver Warner,

Secretary of State, was called upon for a response, but had left the tent, and the sentiment was passed over.

After the performance of the "Star Spangled Banner" by the band, the next regular toast was given as follows: "Practical education and the industrial arts; their seeds were sown in America by the Pilgrims who had to labor or starve."

To respond to this, Dr. Geo. B. Loring, of Salem, was called upon. He was received with applause, and responded in an eloquent manner, which was loudly applauded by the audience.

SPEECH OF DR. LORING.

Mr. President, and Ladies and Gentlemen:

I owe you all an apology for making an attempt to speak at this time and on such an occasion. I sympathize most warmly with the Secretary of the Commonwealth in his flight from this tent. He had been notified, only on his entrance to this place, that he was expected to respond to a sentiment, for which every man should desire careful and ample preparation. It is not a mere impulse, a sudden inspiration, that will enable any one, even the most devoted and admiring citizen of Massachusetts, to set forth in suitable phrase the high qualities and attainments of this honored Commonwealth. Such a subject is worthy of, and is entitled to, the most careful thought and consideration. The apology of the Secretary is my apology. I was not aware that I was expected to say one word — strange as it may seem to some of you — on this occasion, and I came here entirely unprepared to reply to a sentiment which involves the largest knowledge of the industry of our State as developed in the days of our ancestors as well as our own. But I could not fail to respond in some form; for I should be untrue to the blood which flows in my veins, did I fail to appear at this time on Captain's Hill, and to respond for the industry and enterprise of my ancestors, and for the Puritan Commonwealth which they founded. For I cannot forget, sir, that the first contest which took place in the Pilgrim colony, resulted in two lines of inheritance in this State in which the gentleman opposite (Mr. Standish) and myself have a personal interest, and which decided for us our lineage. While he claims descent from Myles Standish, I claim descent from John Alden, from him who vanquished the great captain on the fair and flowery field of love, and decided that the lovely Priscilla should be my ancestor and not his. My grandmother's name was Alathea Alden,— a Puritan name in every respect, and an Old Colony name; — if not, let any woman here bring forward one that is, and let any man find one in his ancestry if he can. And hence it is that I should be false to the blood which flows in my veins, did I fail to respond to your sentiment as best I may. And more than this. The occupation which Myles Standish adopted after he left his fields of conquest, has an especial claim upon me. I understand that he was a Massachusetts farmer, an early representative of that industry which lay at the foundation of our ancient prosperity, and which is so important to us now. He was one of those, who, having, in their hour of need, availed themselves of the sandy store-houses of the Indians, made an honest endeavor to cultivate these hill-sides, as their part of the important service required by a new colony. The example they set was a good one. The people who have followed it have clothed themselves with honor and prosperity. And so as an American citizen, I believe in Myles Standish and his Pilgrim associates, who, having performed good service with their swords, turned their attention to their own acres, and fixed a system of agriculture, and independent and intelligent landholding here, which is the pride and the peculiar prerogation of our people. Upon this foundation they built the fabric of their education, — that admirable co-mingling of polite bearing, moral culture, and practical development, which has become the characteristic of their descendants. And what a true and steady culture was theirs! At its very foundation, they laid the Bible. We were told by the distinguished and eloquent orator of the day, that Myles Standish had three old Bibles and three new muskets. He was indeed well armed for the service of life. As he fought and as he toiled, on whatever field he applied his powers, he cultivated his religious nature, believing that without this man builded all in vain. The inspiration of that inspired volume went with himself and his sturdy companions everywhere, and sustained and warmed them on their path endowing fame. It was their daily companion. And I turn often with supreme delight to that page of an ancient Bible on which one of my ancestors has recorded that he diligently perused its chapter more than sixty times in thirty years. The impression made by such familiarity upon the minds of our fathers is not yet lost upon us. They read but few lighter books. They had but few. They read no newspapers. They had none. Perhaps the gentleman who preceded me, will consider that in this they were fortunate. But, however this may be, it was on religious culture that they built the entire structure of their education, and advanced them to that development of every branch of knowledge and industry which has made this Commonwealth what it is. They were indeed scholars who were engaged in this early colonial work of education. They came from the classical schools of England, and brought the Bible and the classics with them. They knew well what study is, and what education is; and Bradford and Carver and Winslow and Brewster had been graduated at the great colleges of England, and they brought here their taste for letters which, thank God, has not yet died out in our beloved Commonwealth. They were scholars; and when they landed on these shores, their first service was to establish that kind of mental culture here, which has done more to give Massachusetts her power in the nation, than all her industrial arts, and all her achievements on the field or in council. They were scholars; and while their hearts warmed over their college, they forgot not moreover the demands of popular education, true ever to the thought that upon an educated people alone can the foundations of a free republic securely rest. And this is indeed the secret of their power. I honor these pilgrims of Plymouth for their sturdy thought, their intellectual culture, and their liberal sentiments. They believed in and demanded religious toleration. And they left it for the other line of my ancestors — who, I think, have done their part to make Essex County illustrious — to exercise another kind of religious fervor, and to send Roger Williams to Rhode Island, and the dissenting Browns back to England, because their religious views were intolerable, while they themselves held their hands open at all times for all faiths and all religions. It was religious fervor which gave Plymouth an existence, — it was religious tolerance which gave her an immortality.

It is not surprising that the planting of Plymouth on such a foundation of education, religion, toleration, and practical wisdom should outshine all similar events in history. It is not surprising that Plymouth and her institutions should have outlived all similar cotemporaneous events, and have produced an imperishable influence in the history of the country. While Jamestown has decayed, and the places which knew its founders know their race no more; while the systems of the Dutch settlers of New York, against whom Myles Standish carried on his first conflict, and who, the historian Graham says, were unable to cope with the stern qualities developed by the trials at Plymouth, have faded away before the all-conquering institutions of the Pilgrim; while the empire of Lord Baltimore has vanished, and the social and civil system which John Locke planted in the Carolinas has disappeared,— the power of the separatist, of the single-hearted and liberal-minded men of Plymouth, who founded here a commonwealth, upheld by a great faith, and led by a great Captain, has gone on conquering and to conquer. And this was their practical work, in which they felt that in all their conflicts with evil, and their contests with ignorance, it was the duty of those who founded a State to develop alike its material prosperity, and to cultivate the mind and heart and Conscience of the people. And this is the Massachusetts of to-day.

In granting, as you have, to the great Captain who lies buried beneath this sod, the practical power of establishing the sovereignty of the Commonwealth, and the practical intelligence of a cultivator of these acres, and a valuable servant of the colony, you have set forth what a true citizen was in the olden time, and what the best of the citizens of Massachusetts are in our day. I think we all believe in the law of life adopted by Myles Standish, — a separatist faith, a hard, industrious, prosperous, and productive life, and in so much of the military arm as will render it impossible for any man to conceive that he can defy the State with impunity. He was as good a citizen as he was captain; and I agree with the orator of the morning, therefore, that he has left behind him an example of cultivated military genius, and of usefulness to the Commonwealth, worthy of all imitation; and I am sure he would have prided himself as much upon his citizenship, as upon the zeal with which he slew the hostile Indians roaming those primeval forests. I see him now, with the honors of his military service won on the great battle-fields of Europe, a simple citizen in this colony, performing on this shore his daily toil, a warrior to-day, a farmer to-morrow, and ever ready to serve his people in any capacity, a pillar of the church and the State alike, an example for the brave and true in all time. I give you therefore, in closing: The first great civil chieftain of the country,—may the lesson which he taught guide our leaders in all time to come.

Applause followed Dr. Loring's speech.

The President then said, "The next toast is, 'Captain's Hill; it speaks to-day in all its pride,' and I have the honor of introducing to you Mr. Justin Winsor, a citizen of Duxbury formerly, and now at the head of the Boston Public Library."

To this Mr. Winsor responded thus:—

CAPTAIN'S HILL.

A tumult of scorn swept wild through the skies,
Till the echoes were crazed with the taunting replies,
And the valleys looked up with a mute surprise.

It swelled from the Jungfrau's icy steep,
From Jura's wall of stupendous sweep,
From Pilate mirrored in Geneva's deep;—

From where along the Grampian verge
Ben Lomond saw the sea emerge;
Where Snowdon weltered in vapory surge.

'T was heard amid our Northern folk,
When Katahdin to Chocorua broke,
And Greylock all his echoes woke.

Where Lookout stands, a host beside,
Bore off the tumult far and wide,
Till remotest Shasta met the tide.

And thus commingled scoff and mock
Of forest peak and scarréd rock
In one reverberating shock.

Down on a sandy shore there lay
The guileless cause of this riotous fray, —
Our Captain's Hill, — it speaks to-day!

Had the clouds vouchsafed to its summit bare
A vapory cap, 't were then and there
Its scorn had flung it high in air.

Sturdy and true as its hero's soul,
It heard the bantering echoes roll,
And burst in its pride beyond control: —

"There are solider ribs than mine, I know,
And crowns compact of eternal snow,
But where has story a surpassing glow?

"The rugged scarps of the Switzer's land
For monuments of Freedom stand,
But this, around, is the Mayflower's strand!

"All time shall know how by yonder head,
Whose sand-hills loom over the briny bed,
The Bible was kissed and the compact said: —

"Most fateful day which the world e'er saw!
When that scroll was signed with nameless awe
Of the stern omnipotence of law!

"And then, Ben Lomond, with thy lore,
I'll match thee on this storied shore
In tales to laugh at or weep o'er.

"Here at my feet the waves outspread
To where with more than an army's tread
The Pilgrims' struggling band was led.

"And they were weak, as I am small;
But death at its terriblest cannot appal,
If the ranks close up as the weaker fall.

"If Fate claimed half the Insatiate Throne,
Could spare enough for the world to own,
In heart and soul and sinew and bone.

"Mark yonder hero in his leathern hose!
There were times in Flanders, Spanish foes
Skipped as his warring fury rose.

"And yonder stripling, lithe and tall!
Who does not know? aye, each and all
Priscilla's 'Prithee,' to her willing thrall.

"My captain, you'll believe me, friends,
As he drummed his hilt with his finger ends,
Outflanked for once, then vowed amends.

"Proud Lookout, too, what fame thou know'st,
When Hooker scaled with cloudy host, —
I glory in your martial boast.

"But did n't my army, six souls strong,
With doughty Myles, put down the wrong,
Maintain the right, and keep it long?

"And thou, hoar Shasta of the west!
Thou scann'st afar the miners' quest;
Know'st not this land is with fruitage blest?

"We 've shades as classic as the Cam's;
We 've brawn to buffet life's hard jams;
And what is more — we 've Duxbury clams.

"And over the Thump Caps the pinkstern knows
The cod will bite if my gulley shows
Straight in the range of the Gurnet's Nose.

"And now, ye summits lost in cloud!
I 'm little, monarchs, but I 'm proud;
To God alone, my Captain bowed."

And so it spoke, as it speaks to-day,
And felt the better for having its say,
And so may we all feel, now and for aye.

The next regular toast was:—

"Rose Standish, the type of womanly sacrifice: her mantle has fallen on American women"

To this, Rev. E. E. Hale responded as follows:—

RESPONSE OF REV. E. E. HALE.

It is certainly quite time, Mr. President, and ladies and gentlemen, that something should be said about Rose Standish and the women who came with her. Rose Standish is a little forgotten when we talk of Priscilla Mullens, or whatever her name may be. (Laughter.) The truth is, the women who came out in the Mayflower solved the problem of emigration. I give that fact to the lady editors, who do not seem to me to make as much use of it as I think they would be wise to do. The effort to settle North America to the northward of the Gulf of Mexico had been made again and again, and yet again and again, and yet again and again, for a century, and had failed. The Huguenots had made it and had failed; the Spaniards had made it and had failed; the French had made it in Canada, they had made it again in Carolina, and they had failed; Gosnold had made it and had failed; the runagates that came out with Popham had made it and had failed; the people who settled at Jamestown had made it and, as we think, they had failed. As my distinguished friend in front of me said in my hearing, they failed till the day came when the cavalier found out that the Puritan was his master; until that great moment, even Jamestown was a failure. The failure was steady, sir, from 1492 till 1620; the attempt to colonize the North

American continent, north of Florida, was a failure; and why? It was a failure because always, — when Ralph Lane came over, when the Huguenots came over, when John Smith came over, when Gosnold came over, the men came over alone. With the first winter they were inevitably disappointed, and in the next spring they returned to England. Ralph Lane returned to England and his men; Popham and his men returned to England. Gosnold returned to England with his men the very year they came. And why did they return to England? They returned to England because they had not brought their homes with them; because their Rose Standishes stayed at home, while our Rose Standish came here, though she came here to die. It was the women of Plymouth who made the colony of Plymouth the first permanent colony. Rose Standish and the lovely women who came with her (we know they were lovely, because we know their descendants) stand for the success of Protestant colonization. Protestant colonization depends upon the transfer of homes. It is in the transfer of homes that emigration and colonization have succeeded in America. It is only in the transfer of homes that it succeeds, and when my excellent friends who are in charge of the woman's rights movement learn that deeper than constitutions, stronger than churches, more powerful than schools in civilization are the homes of a nation, they will have learned what it seems to me they do not know to-day (applause), and they will have learned the greatest secret of the church government and of the state government of the world. (Applause.)

Myles Standish stands for this, sir; he stands for what is not always understood, the catholicity, the toleration, the generosity of this company of Pilgrims. We hear a great deal about their bigotry. They were men of strong will; they were men who meant to have the right to go forward, they were men, as has been rightly said, who believed in God, and meant to keep their powder dry. Very certainly, they meant to have the world go forward in a particular way, and to that way they consecrated their lives. It is convenient, therefore, for those persons upon whose toes they trod to say they were a narrow, bigoted, self-satisfied set of men. The truth is, this little body of Pilgrims, who settled here in the region around this hill, embraced much more than the church which had been formed in England, was then transferred to Leyden, and then removed here. It embraced such come-outers as Myles Standish. It took in men that did not belong to that church. It took them in with the toleration, with the generosity, with the catholicity which belonged to the character and ought to belong to the church of the new-born people. It is on this catholicity, this generosity to all comers, that the American republic was founded; it is on the same generosity that its prosperity depends to-day. And when you hear one schemer or another talk of leaving out in the cold the men of this lineage or that, of this creed or that, when you hear them talk of America's standing by itself, saying to the rest of the world, "hands off," or "stand back," you hear people talk who do not know anything of the principles of Plymouth Rock, or of the foundation that here was laid.

Myles Standish, himself not a member of their church company, represents that principle of toleration in American history.

It is to this tolerance, indeed, exhibited among their successors, that I owe the pleasure of being present to-day. I am in the midst, say, in round numbers, of 562 descendants of the Pilgrims, myself being the only one among them in whose veins there runs not a drop of Pilgrim blood. (Laughter.) In the last Pilgrim celebration that I attended, on the 225th anniversary of the landing at Plymouth Rock, I chanced to be in the society of a venerable matron who had well informed herself in the history of this matter, and I ventured to say that my only plea for Pilgrim ancestry was based on my hope that it would prove that my venerated ancestor, Madam Pepper, belonged to a Pilgrim family. It is to the blood of that lady that I owe the coolness of disposition which has served me well in trying exigencies. I said I knew she was not in the Mayflower, but I hoped it might yet prove she was in the Fortune, or in the Ann. But I found jesting on this subject dangerous. With a look of perfect iciness she asserted that could not be; that no Pepper ever came over in the Ann, the Fortune, or the Mayflower. It is dangerous joking on such subjects here, sir. They all have their genealogy, — not in the first pages of their Bibles; no, — they have it in their heads. They all of them know from whom they descended; and all the persons around here would say as my friend said, that they knew there was no person named Pepper in either the Ann, the Fortune, or the Mayflower. Since then, I know that I have no right to stand on Pilgrim Rock or Captain's Hill, except on this broad catholicity of the Pilgrim forefathers. Why, you are not in the same boat with me, Mr. President. Your venerated and distinguished relative has made immortal for us the faces of the Pilgrims upon the canvas in the hall yonder. He has shown us the pensive beauty of Rose Standish. He has shown us the manliness of her husband. He has shown us Bradford and the rest of them, in their manner, as they were, and I am sure there is not one of us here but who, looking back upon them in fancy, is guided by the genius of a Sargent in his reproduction of the scene. What is more, there is not one of our friends here but, as I have been speaking, has rehearsed the number of these ladies from whom they themselves descended. We are seven generations from those people. Each of us has two parents, four grandparents, and eight great-grandparents; and by an easy calculation you will see that in the seven generations past, one may have one hundred and twenty-eight great, great, great, etc., grandfathers and grandmothers in the Mayflower, only that, unfortunately, there were but one hundred and one persons there. My charming friend at my side is descended from them all, — she unites all their graces and virtues. My distinguished friend opposite, the treasurer of the Commonwealth as long as the Commonwealth could command his services, is descended from thirty-eight; the lady on your left from sixty-seven; your friend in line with her, from twenty-three. I am, alas, descended from not one! Yet, sir, I have no doubt that my ancestors did their best. (Laughter.) I am not well acquainted with them. They were not a class of people who left their record behind them. They were, I do not doubt, brave men, pure women; but they were not received on board the Mayflower. Since I have sat here, I have pictured to myself their manly procession, their womanly beauty, as they waited on the pier at Plymouth, in southwestern England, for the day when the Mayflower should be sighted at the signal-station, and when she should come up the bay. She leaves Delft-haven; she passes the dangers of the English Channel and comes to Old Plymouth, the farthest port in southwestern England. "Methinks I see her now, the Mayflower of a forlorn hope, freighted with the prospects of a distant State, and bound across the unknown sea." She comes up Plymouth Bay; one hundred and twenty-eight of my ancestors, sir, — sixty-four men and sixty-four women, — are waiting upon the pier, with their passage-tickets in their hands, requesting to be received on board; and at the gangway, with military precision, there stands the sentinel. It is Myles Standish, — afterwards to be the hero of the little company. He looks upon their faces; he sees what may come from them to the old colony in its time; but he looks back upon the hampered vessel, and to the oldest of my ancestors of that day, sir, he says: "You are a handsome man, but you can't come in." (Laughter and applause.) It is only to that great misfortune of that hour, sir, that I owe the disgraceful position which I hold before you now. (Renewed laughter.) I am not acquainted with the facts, I say; I am obliged to draw upon my imagination; and my political friends know that when you have no facts in the blue-books, your imagination is an excellent substitute. I am obliged to draw on my imagination for my facts; but I believe in that sad hour, when they saw the Mayflower leave the shores of Plymouth in England to come across the waters here and establish the New Plymouth, those men and women devoted themselves to American colonization; and so soon as they heard that Winthrop, Dudley, and the rest, were on the way, those sixty-four gallant men and sixty-four gallant women, possessed with the impression of the beauty of Rose Standish upon the deck, and the manliness of Myles Standish as he stood beside her, consecrated themselves to the determination that they would follow the founders of the little State. They remained only ten years in England, and devoted those years to doing what they could to establish the lesser colony of the Bay.

THE PILGRIM MOTHERS.

BY S F. STREETER.

The Pilgrim Mothers! where are they?
Their frames are dust, their souls in heaven;
Yet shall their memory pass away,
Nor praise to their good deeds be given?
"Teach infant lips to sing their name,
(Ten thousand ready tongues reply;)
And give their noble acts to fame;
Tho' now in silent dust they lie!"

They severed fond affection's chain,
And looked and listened o'er and o'er,
On forms they might not see again,
To voices they might hear no more;
Then, tore their bleeding hearts away,
From peaceful homes beyond the sea;
Where they had passed their childhood's day,
Yet where the SPIRIT was not free.

No HOME for them — that magic word,
Which, fraught with love, and joy, and rest,
Whenever and wherever heard,
Unseals pure fountains in the breast;
No home for them — for far away
The dwellings of their kindred stood;
Beyond the swellings ocean's play,
Far from their forest solitude.

They sought a strange and wintry shore,
Yet love burned brightly in their breast;
They shrank not when the mourners bore
The weary spirits to their rest;
And oft, when from a savage tongue,
Pealed wildly forth the battle cry,
They to their trusting children clung,
And calmly gave themselves to die.

O man, boast not of thy lion-heart!
Tell not of proud, heroic deed!
Have we not seen thy vaunted art
Fail in the deepest hour of need?

But, woman's courage! 't is more deep,
More strong than heart of man can feel —
To save her little ones that sleep,
She bares her bosom to the steel.

Daughters of them who, long ago,
Dared the dark storm, and angry sea,
And walked the desert way of woe,
And pain, and trouble, to be FREE!
Oh, be like them! like them endure!
And bow beneath affliction's rod;
Like them be humble, mild and pure —
In joy and sorrow look to God.

Baltimore, 1843.

The next toast was, "The first and the last Surveyors of the Cape — The last has enabled us to pay our tribute to-day to the first."

It was responded to by Hon. Josiah Quincy, who in a pleasant and facetious address deprecated the growing custom of speech-making, urging as his reason for this action that they could not find any record of the Pilgrims' public speaking.

The next sentiment was: —

"Roger Williams, the companion of the pilgrims, the apostle of soul-liberty."

This was responded to as follows by the Rev. Dr. Caswell, president of Brown University:

As a descendant of the pilgrims, I am here to-day to honor those noble pioneers of Christianity and civilization on these shores. But, Mr. President, I came to hear, and not at all to speak. I came to look in reverence upon the spot, which is this day consecrated to the memory of "Captain Myles Standish," the able and dauntless military leader of that little band of exiles.

But why do we honor the Pilgrims? For their heroic virtues, their unflinching devotion to truth and duty, their never-failing and sublime trust in God. The world has seen but few examples of Christian faith and endurance so illustrious as theirs. Amid sickness and sufferings and dangers that might well appal ordinary men and women, and drive them to despair, they remained steadfast and unmoved in their confidence, — "Strong in the Lord, and in the power of his might." This, it seems to me, was their great distinction from other men and other women. In this they hold a proud preëminence. But what can be said in praise of them that has not been said a hundred times already? Suffice it to say, that their principles and their example formed the basis of New-England character. They sowed the precious seed, which, in all parts of the land, has borne fruits an hundred-fold to the honor of piety, and justice, and patriotism. It is hardly too much to say that their principles, propagated in their descendants and through them, permeating and moulding public opinion, have, at length, after more than a century of conflict, made us a nation of freemen, in which there breathes not a single slave.

But, Mr. President, the sentiment which you have given me calls upon me to speak of Roger Williams. We honor his memory in Rhode Island. And I am glad to know that the time is long past since his name was held in dishonor in Massachusetts. With the Plymouth brethren, Williams always maintained the most friendly relations. To some of the leading men in the Massachusetts Bay, he was warmly attached. In his bitter exile he takes evident pleasure in speaking of Governor Winthrop as his "loving friend."

Roger Williams was a statesman as well as a Christian. He saw, probably, more clearly than any man of his times, — and what comparatively few men saw at all, — the necessity of an entire and absolute separation between church and state. He maintained that in all matters of religious concernment, the conscience must be free, — there must be, what he called, "soul-liberty." Every man must be left free to worship God according to the dictates of his own conscience. The civil magistrate must exercise no control and impose no restraint. This was the distinctive feature of his polity with regard to church and state. This, also, was perhaps the chief heresy which made him obnoxious to the rulers of the Massachusetts Bay, and led to his banishment. That event of unhappy memory occurred nearly two hundred and fifty years ago. The ideas of civil and religious liberty, thank God, have made great progress since that time. Who now, in this broad land, stands up to contest with Roger Williams that great principle of religious liberty, which he was the first to promulgate? Among Protestants, we may answer, not one. We here, on this consecrated ground, honor his memory. The nation honors it. The friends of religious liberty in all lands honor it. By common consent, the name of Roger Williams stands to-day among the illustrious names of history.

As a matter of tardy justice to the memory of her

distinguished founder, the State of Rhode Island has recently placed an imposing marble statue of him in the national capitol. It is purely ideal, as no authentic portrait of him is known to exist. But it finely symbolizes the character of the man, — the humility and benevolence of the Christian, the self-reliance and firmness of the pioneer, the dignity and wisdom of the statesman.

As yet, no commemorative monument honors him in the city which he founded. We hope the reproach of ingratitude will not long rest upon those who have so largely entered into his labors and who are so justly proud of their inheritance. It is to be hoped that your good example of to-day may act as a salutary incentive to us.

The next sentiment was: "The Seeds of Civil and Religious Liberty, — planted on our sterile soil by our Pilgrim Fathers, they have brought forth a harvest in which all Christian sects find an inheritance." Rev. Dr. A. A. Miner made an eloquent response.

SPEECH OF DR. MINER.

Mr. President, and Ladies and Gentlemen:

It is but little I have to say, on so short a notice; and at this late hour, brief is the time it would be proper for me to employ. It is not without misgivings I rise at all to respond to the sentiment you have read, as my faith has considerably overflowed the Puritan boundaries. This misgiving was not a little increased by a jocose remark of the gentleman (Mr. Quincy) who has just addressed you, and who may be supposed to be authority in such matters. Riding up Captain's Hill this morning, he said to me and my venerable friend Dr. Neale, who sits before me, that he did not see what business either of us had here. But as Dr. Neale has managed somehow to come in, and as his shoulders are broader than mine, I have followed in his wake. His "Communion," though "close," embraces me, and mine embraces everybody. It may be that this is the door through which the gentleman himself (Mr. Quincy) has entered.

I have, however, one or two things to say for myself. In the first place, I am a descendant of Captain Myles Standish. It is true, I am compelled to rest this claim on somewhat peculiar grounds. George Macdonald, one of the most popular authors, perhaps, at present, among the literary men of Scotland, in one of the most exquisite little poems known to our language, gives the lineage of an infant in the following unique and succinct style: —

"Where did you come from, baby dear?
Out of the everywhere, into here."

Now, as I have the authority of uncorrupted tradition, strengthened by a proximate memory, that I started life an infant, I too may claim to have come from "out of the everywhere into here," and so to have descended in a right line from Myles Standish.

In the second place, though a heretic, judged from the Puritan stand-point, I am a legitimate successor of the Puritans, as regards their claims of personal right to worship God and interpret his word according to the dictates of their own consciences. It is true, "they builded better than they knew." What they claimed for themselves, but had not learned to concede to others, has come to be embodied in institutions. Their private prerogative has come to be recognized as a public principle, and men now seek to draw near to God in the light of the best they know of him. Thus do the principles of righteousness come to be embodied in the understanding and the heart.

If the business of the church were to ticket us for the kingdom of heaven as we were ticketed for Duxbury this morning, the Roman Catholic church could do the work quite as well, perhaps, as any other. But if the business of the church is to fortify the human soul with the principles of justice, integrity, humility, and trustful patience, and to temper and kindle it by the sovereign power of divine love; and if this bringing of a soul into communion with God and making it a law unto itself, is saving it, then the church that best does this, that brings God nearest, that most magnifies his love, that knits the human soul most strongly to him and most controls it by that love which is the "fulfilling of the law," is the best. Thus judged, the Romish church holds a low place; and Roman*ism*, though under Protestant names, is little better. Now, Puritanism, for itself, stands on the right of individual judgment; and we, for ourselves, Puritanism consenting or resisting, stand on the same right, — the right to be a heretic, — the right to show that man's heresy is God's orthodoxy. This private right has become public law, and the harvest from Puritan seed has become the common inheritance of the church.

One thing further. We are professedly honoring the Puritans and their church fidelity. Honor higher than can be embodied in words, would be bestowed by imitating what was noblest in their church life, — fidelity to the best they knew. Churches may put on all the external appearances of thrift and religious zeal, and at the same time remain utterly worldly, fashionable, and self-seeking. I yield to no man in my respect for a truly Christian church. But those churches which take a bottle in one hand and a ballot in the other, and deposit the latter to perpetuate the dominion of the former, present very doubtful claims to any man's respect. For myself, I prefer to be voted out of such a church to being voted into it; and if I must go to heaven with its ticket of indorsement pinned to my garments, I would ask some heretic to cover it with a patch of simple unhypocritical worldliness, that divine grace might not be put to any unnecessary strain in receiving me. Not until we can rise, under our measure of light, to the grand fidelity of the Puritans under theirs, shall we truly honor them; and not until we vote as we think, and live and act as we vote, will God be honored and man be blest.

The next regular toast was then announced as follows: "The Pilgrim Colonies, — their records have the simple poetry of mythology and the philosophic truth of history."

To this toast Dr. Shurtleff responded. His remarks were full of beauty and historic interest.

REMARKS OF DR. SHURTLEFF.

Mr. President: —

Coming here at this time out of respect to the Pilgrim forefathers of Duxbury and their worthy descendants, it would certainly be much more agreeable to me to be a silent listener to the pleasant words of others, than to consume any of the time of this interesting occasion by being a speaker. But having a good share of Pilgrim blood coursing through my veins, perhaps as much as any one present, it would seem wrong, after receiving your kind invitation, to let my aversion to public speaking prevent my responding to what you have just proposed.

What you, sir, have just now said about the records of the Pilgrim colonies is perfectly correct. They possess all that you have attributed to them, and even more: But it is of very little consequence on this occasion what the words of a toast are, for the sentiments that pervade all of us to-day cannot be otherwise than concerning the Pilgrim forefathers of New England. We who esteem ourselves happy in being descended from these worthies, always rejoice in an opportunity to pay deserved tribute to their memories by rehearsing their virtues and estimable characteristics. We consider it our bounden duty to communicate to our children and successors those things worthy of remembrance which we have learned from our fathers. Now, sir, with what you and others gathered together around this hospitable board have so well said, nothing of this has been neglected; nor have the mighty deeds of valor that were performed of old by our venerated ancestors been forgotten. How could we on an occasion with such interesting purposes as this in view, forget these worthy people? We are now on their own ground, and in sight of the scenes of their early endeavors. The places which they once trod, and where they dwelt and labored, are before and around us. Every object that meets our view reminds us of what has transpired in the past, and of the historic characters who have achieved so much for their posterity.

The special object of this present gathering on Captain's Hill — the consecration of the ground on which we hope soon to see reared an enduring monument to the Pilgrims' captain — cannot but awaken within us many memories of the past which must necessarily renew associations of the most pleasant character, and carry us back to the ancient days when the Pilgrim worthies were here in the flesh, as they undoubtedly now are in the spirit. In the selection of a site for the memorial, you have been singularly fortunate. It is most prominently situated, and is discernible from all the Pilgrim surroundings, and moreover, was early set apart for the use of the brave captain by his grateful contemporaries. Standing on it, as we now do, we recognize the appropriateness of the place. From its lofty eminence, hallowed by the remembrance of the valiant Captain and venerated Elder, scenes of the greatest interest open to our view. At our feet we can distinctly trace the vestiges of these fathers and of their humble abodes. We can drink to-day from their never-failing springs of living water, and partake of products raised in their own fertile fields. At no great distance from the shores that nearly surround this delightful peninsula, we can distinguish the very place where, just within view of the promised land, rode the renowned May Flower and its little colony of self-exiled pilgrims. Very near can be seen the delightful island which first gave rest and safety and comfort to these weary people, and where, under the shelter of the hospitable rock that even now marks the sacred spot, they passed their first Christian Sabbath in New England. From this, your chosen site, can be seen all the noted landmarks of the Pilgrim history.

While we survey these ancient scenes and former abodes of the Pilgrim fathers, we should consider ourselves exceedingly fortunate and happy that so much knowledge of what concerned them has been preserved on written and printed pages, and that reminiscences have also been transmitted to us by truthful tradition, most sacredly passed down from generation to generation of the descendants of the first comers. But when I say "truthful traditions," Mr. President, I do not mean to class with them any foolish and vague impossibilities, that neither heighten, in our estimation, those whose memory we should revere, nor give us ideas of what did not take place. History and Ideality can keep closely together, and strengthen and beautify each other; but Truth should be their handmaid and ever-present companion. The positive historian must, and always will, doubt traditionary lore, because, in it error frequently supplants and eradicates truth, diverts reality from its direct course, and very sadly perverts history.

However truthful record has been respecting the history of our pilgrim ancestry, tradition has been greatly at fault. Truth and propriety have been set aside, and error and frivolity have prevailed. But, fortunately, the written and printed records speak louder and stronger than wide-mouthed tradition, and all is safe. In the laudable contention of claiming for ancestors the honor of being the first to place foot upon the Plymouth rock, tradition has most signally failed. Both sexes have set up pretensions to this distinction, and some of the most excellent of the May Flower passengers have to be set aside because, having other engagements aboard ship, they did not happen to be of the first boat-load that reached the shore at the water-side of their new-found haven of rest in New Plymouth.

The first three marriages in the colony were of persons all of whom were passengers of the Mayflower: Edward Winslow married widow Susanna White; John Howland married Elizabeth Tilley, and John Alden married Priscilla Mullens. These marriages took place when all the colonists dwelt on the two sides of Leyden Street, between Burying Hill and the water side in Plymouth, and sometime before Edward Winslow brought over the three heifers and one bull,— the first neat cattle in the colony,— in the Ann, in March, 1624. Therefore, the tradition that Howland married a daughter of Governor Carver is not true; nor would Alden have required any animal for his newly-married wife to ride a few rods, especially when there were none in the colony larger than a good-sized dog, or goat, or respectable pig.

The redoubtable actions of the brave Standish, the excellencies of Alden, Southworth, Brewster, Collier, and innumerable other worthies, we can all believe, because they are matters of record, and we notice them daily exemplified by their posterity. Let us continue to emulate these examples of excellence and worth; and as the Standish memorial shall rise, stone upon stone, let our determination be strengthened to be guided by instructions which they left for our good.

Far away, sir, in the old borough of Boston, in Lincolnshire, which furnished so many good colonists for our Boston, there stands a noble old church-edifice known as St. Botolph's, with an extraordinarily tall tower. There formerly worshipped many saintly persons whose lives terminated in New England. It is said of the estimable John Cotton, of Boston, that while he was vicar of St. Botolph's, he kept during dark nights a light upon that tower to guide the wayfarers over the bogs and moors and fens of Lincolnshire; and it is likewise said that when Cotton came to New England the light of St. Botolph's went out. Be this as it may, certainly a new light was transferred to America which served here as a most brilliant luminary. May we not hope that our memorial may tower up on high like old St. Botolph's, and serve not only as a safe guide to the weary mariner and wayfarer, but also be a landmark, from whose lofty top shall be pointed out the foot-paths of our fathers, and, recalling the remembrance of the past, excite to the best endeavors the sons and daughters of the Pilgrim stock.

The exercises were concluded by "Auld Lang Syne" by the band.

Owing to the extreme uncertainty of the railroad being finished in season to transport the guests, the committee, with much regret, were obliged to withhold many invitations till the last moment, which rendered it impossible for some of the distinguished invited guests to be present. Many letters of sympathy with the cause were received, but with regrets that intervening engagements would prevent their presence on the occasion. Lord Parker was present on the grounds during the day, remaining till the exercises were over, and showing much interest, but carefully avoided being called out. Lord Walter Campbell sent his regrets, as did many distinguished citizens who would, if possible, have been present. Extracts from the following letters show the great interest in the Memorial to Standish, and the press of the country have universally and strongly favored this tribute to the memory of the old hero. The generals and other officers of the army, as well as the privates of the Grand Army of the Republic, all approve of erecting a monument to the memory of the first commissioned officer of the United States, and some of the best soldiers, as well as many distinguished civilians, are already members of the Association. The expenses of the festival were borne by the citizens of Duxbury, who, are deserving of much credit for their perseverance and energy in trying to make so large an audience comfortable under such disadvantageous circumstances, and without any expense to the Memorial Association.

Five acres of land for the monument has been donated by the owner of the Standish farm, at the request of the Standish heirs, and ten acres more of adjoining land has been placed by him in the hands of the treasurer of the Association, to be by them assessed and sold for betterments, if, in the opinion of the directors, the erection of the monument shall in any manner benefit pecuniarily the balance of the Standish farm, -- if not, the same is to be re-deeded to him.

To George Bradford, Thomas Chandler, and Charles H. Chandler, Selectmen, and other town officers and citizens of Duxbury, the Association is much obligated for contributions and assistance, in entertaining the guests, as well as for their universally expressed sympathy for the memory of Myles Standish.

LETTERS

From the President of the United States.

"I am heartily with your Association, in sympathy with any movement to honor one who was as prominent in the early history of our country as Myles Standish; but my engagements are such that I regret I am unable to promise to be present at the dedication in August.

"With many thanks for your kindness in sending me the invitation, I am respectfully yours,

U. S. Grant."

General Sherman writes: "Of course the propositon to erect a monument in sight of Massachusetts Bay, to that stanch old soldier, Miles Standish, meets my hearty approbation, and I should be most happy to assist.

"But I have been away so much that I ought to stay at home," etc.

From General Sheridan.

"I do not know that my engagements will permit of my being present at the time mentioned, but will do so if I can.

"In any event, allow me to assure you of my admiration and respect for the services and sturdy character of the man, and my hearty approval of the object of your Association."

P. H. Sheridan.

"I beg to say that I heartily approve of your intention to erect a Memorial to Captain Standish, and I think there is no more fitting spot than the one you have chosen for that purpose.

"I shall be glad to be with you if possible. Thanking you for your courteous invitation,

"I remain, yours very truly,

"A. E. Burnside."

From General Hooker.

"I regret to state that my engagements for the month of August are such, as to render it impossible for me to join you on that memorable occasion. It is unnecessary for me to say that I deeply sympathize with the object of your meeting. I have been an admirer of the character of Myles Standish from my boyhood up, and would like to be identified with any body of gentlemen engaged in commemorating his great virtues. To me, his civil and military character towers far above his contemporaries, and they, if I mistake not (when history shall be truthfully written), will be made to appear to be the most remarkable body of men that ever lived. Viewed from our present standpoint, in my opinion, they are now entitled to that judgment. It will be a graceful act on the part of our friends, to erect a monument to his memory; but it must not be expected to add to his fame or immortality. Industry, valor, and integrity were regarded as the cardinal virtues of our forefathers, and I hope they will never be held in less estimation by their descendants. One of our gifted poets has happily named 'Plymouth Pock' as the corner-stone of the nation. The superstruction promises to be worthy of the foundation. With great respect, I have the honor to be your friend and servant,

"J. Hooker, *Major-General.*"

"Unexpected engagements will deprive me of the pleasure of accepting your kind invitation for the day. Frequent recurrence to the forming period of national character distinguishes a wise and patriotic people. The incident at Cape Anne in 1625, 'the eager and peremptory demand' of Standish, combined with the 'prudence and moderation' of Governor Conant, exhibit the characteristics, the combination of energy and wisdom, of decision and firmness, which again made the law a century and a half later at Bunker Hill.

"The spirit of self-assertion and independence in 1625, bred that which paralyzed the English Council in 1671, and British arms in 1775; which repeated 'the 19th of April' in 1861, and thwarted British greed in alliance with Southern Slavery. The historical connection is complete.

"Very respectfully, yours,

"J. WINGATE THORNTON."

From Ex-Governor Sprague, of Rhode Island.

"I fear my other engagements will deprive me of the pleasure of mingling with those who meet to honor the sterling character of our ancestor, and call up their deeds for the imitation of the actors of this hour. Express to the Association my sense of the honor done me by their invitation. Associations of men of the present time, who honor men of the past for acts which have redounded to the elevation of those who live subsequently, have the same, or some of the same elements of character themselves, that they honor. We can tell by the public acts of the man, or of communities, whether among them, or in the nation, the word of progress is *Forward!* whether there is a *backward tread.* Men *cannot stand still;* the highest perfection is, *man progressing;* the lowest scale of being is, *man decaying.*

"Very respectfully, yours,

"W. SPRAGUE."

"As a descendant of those who landed on the Plymouth Rock, I feel a special interest in whatever relates to the brave soldier, Captain Myles Standish, by whose sword the little colony was in its infancy defended. I am withheld from attending the ceremony which is to take place on the 17th, by various occupations which take up all my leisure, and must content myself with expressing my satisfaction that it was so fully shown by our late civil war, that those who have inherited from the noble stock of the Pilgrim fathers, the region once defended by his valor, inherit also the courage and resolution which have made his name famous in our history.

"I am, Sir, with great respect, your obedient servant,

W. C. BRYANT."

STANDISH MONUMENT

ON

CAPTAIN'S HILL, DUXBURY.

CHARTER, ORGANIZATION, AND BREAKING GROUND.

LAYING CORNER-STONE,

OCTOBER 7, 1872.

UNDER THE DIRECTION OF THE ANCIENT AND HONORABLE ARTILLERY COMPANY,

By the Grand Lodge of Massachusetts,

AND OTHER ASSOCIATIONS.

PREPARED BY STEPHEN M. ALLEN,

CORRESPONDING SECRETARY OF THE STANDISH MONUMENT ASSOCIATION.

BOSTON:
ALFRED MUDGE & SON, PRINTERS, 34 SCHOOL STREET
1873.

STANDISH MONUMENT

ON

CAPTAIN'S HILL, DUXBURY.

CHARTER, ORGANIZATION, AND BREAKING GROUND

LAYING CORNER-STONE,

OCTOBER 7, 1872.

UNDER THE DIRECTION OF THE ANCIENT AND HONORABLE ARTILLERY COMPANY,

By the Grand Lodge of Massachusetts,

AND OTHER ASSOCIATIONS.

PREPARED BY STEPHEN M. ALLEN,

CORRESPONDING SECRETARY OF THE STANDISH MONUMENT ASSOCIATION.

BOSTON:

ALFRED MUDGE & SON, PRINTERS, 34 SCHOOL STREET.

1873.

STANDISH MONUMENT,

CAPTAIN'S HILL, DUXBURY, MASS.

GEN. HORACE BINNEY SARGENT, PRESIDENT.

NATHANIEL ADAMS, CHAIRMAN OF EXECUTIVE COMMITTEE AND MASTER OF CONSTRUCTION, BOSTON.

FRANCIS STANDISH,
EDWIN ADAMS, } SUPTS. OF CONSTRUCTION, BOSTON.

STEPHEN N. GIFFORD, SECRETARY, DUXBURY.

STEPHEN M. ALLEN, CORRESPONDING SECRETARY, BOSTON.

CHARTER

FROM THE

LEGISLATURE OF MASSACHUSETTS.

By a new Charter, accepted and adopted June 17, 1872, the name of the Association was changed to the "Standish Monument Association," and a meeting held at Duxbury on that day, at 10 o'clock, A. M., was duly organized, and the following officers were elected: —

President. — Gen. Horace Binney Sargent.

Advisory Presidents. — His Excellency Marshall Jewell, Connecticut; Hon. James A. Weston, New Hampshire; Hon. Robert C. Winthrop, Massachusetts; Gen. Joshua L. Chamberlain, Maine; Rev. Dr. George Putnam, Massachusetts; Hon. Alexander H. Rice, Boston; Dr. George B. Loring, Salem; Hon. John H. Clifford, Massachusetts; Gen. A. E. Burnside, Rhode Island; Hon. Nathaniel B. Shurtleff, Boston; Hon. E. S. Tobey, Boston; Hon. Horatio Harris, Boston; Miles Standish, Esq., New York.

Directors. — Hon. Onslow Stearns, Concord, N. H.; Hon. Thomas Russell, Boston; Nathaniel Adams, Boston; Lemuel Miles Standish, Boston; Samuel Little, Boston; Samuel C. Cobb, Dr. Ira L. Moore, Boston; Samuel Loring, Duxbury; Nathan Matthews, Boston; Frederic C. Adams, Kingston; Francis Standish, Boston William Whiting, Boston; Nathan Morse, Boston; Isaac Keene, Duxbury; Jonathan S. Ford, Duxbury; Rev. Josiah Moore,

Duxbury; Dr. James Wilde, Duxbury; Thos. Chandler, Duxbury; Charles H. Chandler, Samuel Atwell, Duxbury; James Ritchie, Boston; Stephen M. Allen, Boston; Edwin Adams, Boston; Edwin C. Bailey, Boston; George Curtis, Stephen N. Gifford, Duxbury; Joseph S. Beal, Kingston; Alden S. Bradford, Kingston; George B. Standish, Duxbury; Alden B. Weston, Duxbury; Elbridge Chandler, Duxbury; Hamilton E. Smith, Duxbury; Oliver Ditson, Boston; Dr. Charles T. Jackson, Boston; Dr. Cushing Webber, Boston; Gen. B. F. Butler, Lowell; Hon. Jonas Fitch, Boston; Hon. Jacob H. Loud, Plymouth; George Bradford, Duxbury; John S. Loring, Duxbury; Harrison Loring, Boston; J. W. Coburn, Boston; Alden Frink, Boston; W. S. Danforth, Plymouth; George W. Wright, Duxbury; Dr. Calvin Pratt, Duxbury; Parker C. Richardson, Duxbury; Job A. Turner, Boston; Joshua M. Cushing, Duxbury; Josiah Peterson, Duxbury; F. P. Sherman, Duxbury; John H. Nickerson, Boston; George Curtis, Boston; William S. Adams, Kingston.

Secretary. — Stephen N. Gifford, Duxbury.

Corresponding Secretary. — Stephen M. Allen, Boston.

Treasurer. — Jacob H. Loud, Plymouth and Boston.

Executive Committee. — Nath'l Adams, Lemuel Myles Standish, Hon. E. S. Tobey, Samuel Little, Francis Standish, James Ritchie, S. M. Allen, Edwin Adams, Jacob H. Loud, Harrison Loring, Job H. Turner, Gen. H. B. Sargent.

Finance Committee. — Horatio Harris, Hon. Alexander H. Rice, Hon. E. S. Tobey, Nathan Matthews, Oliver Ditson, Dr. Geo. B. Loring, Samuel Little, Jacob H. Loud, Nathaniel Adams, Jonathan S. Ford, George B. Standish, Gen. B. F. Butler, Geo. W. Wright, Jonas Fitch, W. S. Danforth, Hon. Nathaniel B. Shurtleff, Rev. Dr. George Putnam, Joseph S. Beal.

After the election the Association partook of a primitive lunch in the old Standish Cottage, and proceeded to the top of Captain's Hill, to break ground for the Monument, which was done in presence of a large, interested crowd of friends and spectators.

After prayer by Rev. Josiah Moore, Gen. H. B. Sargent, the President, introduced the Selectmen of Duxbury, who, through their chairman, in behalf of the town, broke the first earth. The President followed in behalf of the company, and Nathaniel Adams, Esq., as Chairman of the Executive Committee; the officers of Corner Stone Lodge of Freemasons, and the officers of Mattakeeset Lodge of Odd Fellows, followed. An opportunity for the ladies was given, when they joined in and handled the spade in good earnest. The Ancient and Honorable Artillery Company were represented; also the oldest Company of State Militia; also the families of Bradford, Brewster, Phillips, Pryor, Simmons, Allen, Ritchie, and many others of the descendants of the Pilgrims.

It was voted to accept and adopt the Plans of the Monument presented by Alden Frink, Esq., and proceed at once with the work on the Monument. It was also voted that the Secretary be directed to ask from the President of the United States a stone for the first arch of the Monument; and stones for the sides from each of the New-England States, as also stones from each County in Massachusetts, all properly inscribed; also similar stones from each Military Company of the State, with the name properly cut thereon.

LAYING THE FOUNDATION STONE.

August 9, 1872. An informal meeting of the Association was held at Captain's Hill, in presence of Tremont Lodge No. 15, I. O. O. F., of Boston, who were visiting Duxbury. The service of laying the first foundation corner-stone was performed by Nathaniel Adams, Esq., with aid of Edwin Adams, Esq., and Mr. Andrew Northey, in presence of and assisted by the Grand Master of the Order of I. O. O. F., many members of Tremont Lodge, and citizens generally.

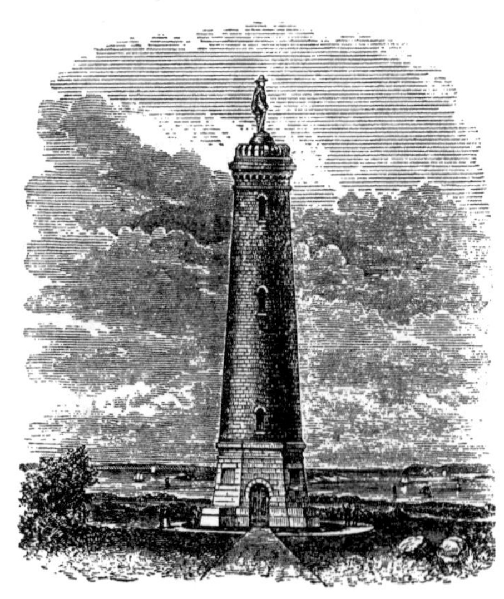

LAYING OF THE CORNER-STONE,

OCTOBER 7, 1872.

FALL FIELD-DAY OF THE ANCIENT AND HONORABLE ARTILLERY COMPANY.

APPROPRIATE HISTORICAL OBSERVANCE.

OLD Mattakeeset was never so overrun with numbers, nor stirred to a greater interest in any celebration, than she is to-day over that attending the laying of the corner-stone of the monument dedicated to the memory of the military defender of the Pilgrim Colony of 1620, Captain Myles Standish. The French Cable celebration of but three years ago, and the excitement it created in the then quiet town, were comparatively insignificant when placed in comparison with the observances of to-day, considered either in the light of local, State, or national importance.

The Standish Monument Association, of which General Horace Binney Sargent is President, and in which many of the most prominent New Englanders, in public or private life, hold official positions, having completed the foundation and raised the base of the memorial above the surface of *terra firma*, sought the aid of the Most Worshipful Grand Lodge of Freemasons of the Old Bay State to perform the active duties of the ceremony, a request that was happily and promptly responded to by that ancient organization. To give *éclat* to the occasion, and to carry out the celebration in a manner in keeping with the life of the honored subject of the memorial, the healthy presence of the military arm was also sought in the escort and guard of the oldest of our martial organizations, the Ancient and Honorable Artillery Company of Massachusetts, and to-day, the annual fall field-day of that time-honored battalion, was selected as the most appropriate date for the historical commemoration. The Highland School Battalion, of Boston, was also invited as a representative body of the coming defenders of the honor of the State and nation, and Masonic organizations generally were requested to present themselves, as their inclinations dictated.

The preliminaries of the celebration, or rather the outward demonstration in connection with it, may fairly be said to have begun in Boston with the departure of the Ancient and Honorable Artillery Company from its armory in Faneuil Hall. There the members assembled at seven o'clock, to the number of about three hundred and fifty, and at eight o'clock formed in the square, whence, headed by Brown's Brigade Band, the march was taken through Merchants Row, State Washington, Winter, and Tremont Streets to Masonic Temple, where the Grand Lodge awaited their coming. Taking this body of Masonic dignitaries under escort, with their own invited guests, the officers of the Providence Light Infantry, the Ancients proceeded directly to the Old Colony Railroad Station, where a fine train of eight cars awaited their transportation to Duxbury.

The Ancients were officered as follows: —

Captain, Edward Wyman; First-Lieutenant, Walter Everett; Second-Lieutenant, Jarvis D. Braman; Adjutant, Ezra J. Trull; First-Sergeant, Eben R. Frost; Second-Sergeant, Samuel Hichborn; Third-Sergeant, Josiah H. Pickett; Fourth-Sergeant, Andrew G. Smith; Fifth-Sergeant, Wm. R. Bennett; Sixth-Sergeant, Albert S. Haven; Seventh-Sergeant, Warren S. Davis; Eighth-Sergeant, Thomas B. Jordan; Ninth-Sergeant, Eugene H. Sampson; Tenth-Sergeant, Davis W. Bailey; Treasurer and Paymaster, John G. Roberts; Clerk and Assistant-Paymaster, Geo. H. Allen; Quartermaster, Charles S. Lambert; Armorer, Richard M. Barker; Committee of Arrangements, Lieutenant John L. Stevenson, Captain Samuel Talbot, Jr., Lieutenant Charles W. Stevens, Sergeant Vincent La Forme, Sergeant T. B. Jordan.

The ladies of Duxbury appointed a committee of three, consisting of Mrs. Stephen M.Allen, Mrs. Lincoln,and Miss Louise Cowing, to preside at the raising of a large and elegant flag, presented by Major-General B. F. Butler. The flag was thrown to the breeze on the staff of the derrick above the monument, by Mrs. Emma Standish Richmond, daughter of L. Miles Standish, of Boston, just as the first train of cars from Boston arrived at the depot this morning. In behalf of the committee, the chairman, Mrs. Allen, made the following address to Edwin Adams, one of the superintendents of construction: —

"It becomes my pleasant duty, in behalf of my associates and the ladies of Duxbury, to present this flag to the Standish Monument Association, to be this day unfurled and given to the breeze by the hand of a lineal descendant of the sturdy Pilgrim captain, over the grand and majestic work you are doing to perpetuate his memory.

"In this service of pleasure and duty which the ladies of Duxbury have the honor to perform, they have to acknowledge their indebtedness to Major-General B. F. Butler, a member of the Association, who, absent from us to-day, has kindly presented the flag for this purpose, to be placed on the rising memorial of the first commissioned military captain of the colonies. May this noble emblem of our country's honors speak to the hearts of every patriot and citizen, proving to the world that the nation's glory is never diminished by doing justice to private worth, especially to those who, while fighting our battles, were willing to protect our sanctuaries with their lives and fortunes."

The train arrived in Duxbury at 10.30, and the masons and military, as they debarked, were informally received by the townspeople and visitors, who had collected in large numbers in the immediate vicinity. A collation was partaken of in the railroad station by the military and their company, and upon the arrival of a later train with the association and guests, the procession for Captain's Hill was formed in the following order: —

Brown's Brigade Band.
The Ancient and Honorable Artillery Company.
The Grand Lodge of Free and Accepted Masons of Massachusetts,
M. W. Sereno D. Nickerson, Grand Master.
Plymouth Band.
The Corner Stone Lodge of Duxbury.
The Pilgrim Lodge of Plymouth
Delegations from other Masonic Lodges.
Chief Marshal, Colonel Newell A. Thompson.
Aids — Colonel Jonas H. French, Major George O. Carpenter, General

Samuel C. Lawrence, and Major Joseph L. Henshaw.
The President of the Standish Monument Association,
General Horace Binney Sargent,
with the Advisory Presidents — the Directors and other Officers, and
the Committees of that Organization.
Invited Guests of the Association.
Governor Padelford and Staff.
Selectmen and Town Officers of Duxbury.
Military Delegation, in uniform.
The Duxbury Lodge of the Independent Order of Odd Fellows.
The Duxbury Lodge of Good Templars.
Citizens of Duxbury.
A Detachment of the Boston Highland School Regiment, under command
of Captain Horace G. Allen.

After a short march, the procession filed around the site of the monument on the summit of the hill, and the assemblage was called to order by the chief marshal. Brief devotional exercises followed, and General Horace Binney Sargent, President of the Monument Association, then delivered the following address: —

Fellow-Citizens: — To-day, upon this bold headland, which once belonged to Myles Standish, and which has been not more enduring than his fame, we have met together to lay the corner-stone of a monument in honor of the great Puritan captain. In recognition of his noble life, consecrated to the holiest principles of public service, the Most Worshipful Grand Master of the Grand Lodge of Free and Accepted Masons of Massachusetts, with his proper officers, and with all appropriate observances which are of usage with that distinguished brotherhood, will perform this ceremony. In illustration of the time-honored military sentiment of this ancient Commonwealth, and of the vigorous legend which has floated over a hundred battle-fields upon her pure, pale banner, as her citizen soldiery have borne it through smoke and flame in the agony of her glory, her oldest military organization, the Ancient and Honorable Artillery, true to their old renown, provide the escort for our memorial service to the first commissioned military officer of New England. Representatives from every organization of State soldiery, young heroes and martyrs of the coming time, distinguished official visitors from other States, citizens, illustrious in the various paths of social life, dwellers of the inland and dwellers by the sea, assemble on this hill-side to establish a column that shall rise high above the headland and look far out forever over the Atlantic, in lasting commemoration of the trained citizen soldier, whose ashes lie somewhere near our feet, though his grave is lost to memory, and to whom this infant nation, which gratefully recognized his services by granting to him this height of Captain's Hill, owed on many desperate occasions the only chance of life.

Why is it, that, thus, two hundred and fifty-two years since Myles Standish stepped upon this shore, then covered with forests and peopled by savage tribes, we joyfully assemble to pay this long-delayed honor to the fierce English trooper of the Lowland wars, whom God seemed to have forced, through deep misfortune, to seek, in service against the bloody Duke of Alva, that iron training of hand and heart which enabled Myles Standish in after time to defend the saintly Pilgrims? Is it not partly because his mail-clad mantle has fallen on our age?

Republics are said to be ungrateful. We need not go far from the present hour to find some color for this assertion. But the sober second thought of the people is always just. The deep, warm, central heart of the nation does not at the last forget. One century, by grave experience, is sharply reminded of the shortcomings of another. Our civil war has awakened us to these debts of gratitude.

For nearly one hundred years we have endeavored to create a nation. A single confusion of thought, which disturbed the deliberations of our fathers, has impeded their sons. Our fathers, bred under the inconvenience of a somewhat central and personal government, did not all clearly see that the ultimate national authority, whether resting in a monarch or the people, must be definitely and exclusively fixed somewhere, and be recognized by all the governed, as there indisputable and supreme. In the joyous moment of throwing off the chains of monarchy, the fatal peril of partitioning the ultimate supreme authority between the States and the nation, so as to leave the question of supremacy in doubt, was not clearly perceived by all the Revolutionary patriots who framed our present constitution. The madness of the idea, that, in a government, intended to be permanent, a national party, founded on the right of insubordination as its chief corner-stone, could be permitted to exist, was not so evident a hundred years ago. We have been forced to see the necessity of government. The past decade has developed all the miseries that can flow from confounding nationalization with centralization, — from confusing the most vigorous exercise of power, delegated from the people, by the people, for the people, to the agent of the people, with a *personal* government. Civil war has smashed the political heresy out of life, that a national party, not anarchical, can be founded on a doubt as to the ultimate resting-place of national supremacy, or on the right to dispute the national authority on every industrial or social question that may arise. National impotence, culminating in civil war, is the legitimate fruit of a tree, which Madison, Hamilton, and Washington asserted to be poisonous, when the statesmen of South Carolina and Maryland tried to engraft it on our constitution. National vigor has returned to our land, through the old stormy channel of safety. *The citizen soldiers* of the nation have settled the question. After eighty-five years of national wrangling whether the voting arm-bearing millions of the people, or the imaginary beings called States, control this Union, three amendments and a score of statutes are declaratory of the fact, that the nation is master of her own broad quarter-deck. Thanks be to God, we are at last a *Nation!*

The spirit of the age is earnest. The national supremacy being decided, the popular heart is prepared to demand a vigorous execution of law, and to reverence the power behind it. The absorption of a million of men, accustomed to short commands and prompt obedience, into our social life, which has become enervated by excessive, flabby legislation and weak enforcement of the statutes, has infused a spirit of respect for fearless vigor. This respect seeks all modes of expression. Men who have staked their lives on their convictions may be expected to admire earnest honesty. It is this earnestness of purpose, the result of the returning armies and the nation's baptism of fire, — setting her heart aglow, as with pentecostal flame, filling men with noble words and thoughts they did not know, — which is displacing the time-serving politicians, and recognizing the Myles Standish of each perilous hour, as the honest and vigorous force behind the law. Gratitude to the citizen soldier — recognition of him as worthy of all respect — is a part of the meaning of this special memorial service. We cannot forget that a citizen soldier guarded the cradle of the infant colony two hundred and fifty years ago, and was her trusted servant for half a century of civil life. A citizen soldier led our fathers to victory against the British throne; and though assailed in his lifetime by ungrateful abuse, which he complained of as unjustifiable, even if applied to a notorious defaulter, is remembered as first in war, first in peace, and first in the hearts of his countrymen. To pass by an illustrious example of the fact that events repeat themselves, it was a citizen soldier, humble and poor, of African descent, — so little does glory care for condition, race, or color, — who, torn by shot and shell, writhed into Fort Wagner on his shattered limbs, still bearing your banner aloft into those lurid gates of hell, as if to show to succeeding ages how a citizen of the great republic should serve the motherland, — fearlessly, joyously, as if entering the gates of heaven; devoutly, as before God upon his knees!

Not only to the memory of Myles Standish, as the type of fearless and honest vigor in public service, as soldier and civilian, but also in a reverent spirit of remembrance and grateful honor to the citizen soldiers of New England, from the landing of the Pilgrims to the present hour, do we lay this corner-stone to-day. Fellow-citizens, we thank you for your presence.

Mr. Chairman of the Executive Committee: — My humble task is finished. In behalf and by the orders of the Standish Monument Association, over which I have the honor to preside, I commit the work thus far completed to your able and honored hands.

Mr. Nathaniel Adams, Chairman of the Executive and Building Committees, on being introduced by General Sargent, gave to the Grand Master official custody of the corner-stone in the following words: —

Most Worshipful Grand Master: — The box containing all the documents and other contributions which have been permitted to be placed therein, together with the inscribed plate, has been sealed and is ready to be placed in the cavity prepared for its reception in the bed of the corner-stone. The stone is now ready to be placed in its position in the base course, upon which is to be erected a monument to the memory of that noble man, Myles Standish.

And I have the honor now to place it in your custody, for the purpose of being laid with the solemn and impressive ceremonies of that ancient order of which you are the official head in this Commonwealth.

Grand Master Sereno D. Nickerson made an appropriate and graceful reply in acceptance of the trust, and Hon. N. B. Shurtleff, to whom had been delegated the duty of preparing the plate and the contents of the memorial box to be enclosed in the corner-stone, delivered the box into the possession of the Grand Treasurer, Mr. John McClellan, who read the inscription and a list of the contents, which follow: —

Programme of the Exercises, Oct. 7, 1872; Plate and Proof and other papers of the Association and History of Myles Standish, also a list of Officers of the Association; Acts and Resolves of the State of Massachusetts, 1872; Records of the various Counties of Massachusetts; History of Duxbury; Catalogue of Prince's Library deposited in the Public Library; Catalogue of Harvard College; Catalogue and other papers of Amherst College; Proceedings of the American Antiquarian Society; Papers from Massachusetts Historic-Genealogical Society; Catalogue and Papers from Tufts College; Catalogue and Papers from Brown's University; Silver Plate of one Roster of The Ancient and Honorable Artillery Company; List of Officers and Chaplains Ancient and Honorable Artillery Company; List of Officers and other papers of Massachusetts Charitable Mechanic Association; Adjutant-General's Report of Massachusetts, 1871; Records from the Companies of the Military of the State; Hingham Journal of October 4, 1872; The Commonwealth, Boston, October 5, 1872; Old Colony Memorial, Plymouth, October 3, 1872; Company C,

First Regiment Infantry, M. V. M., Claflin Guard; Concord Artillery and other Military Companies of the State of Massachusetts; Current Newspapers of Massachusetts; Proceedings of the Cable Celebration at Duxbury; many other Documents; a piece of our Forefathers' Rock; a piece of the hearth-stone of the original Myles Standish house, taken from the ruins.

The following is a copy of the metallic plate: —

THE CORNER-STONE
of the
STANDISH MEMORIAL,
in commemoration
of the
character and services of
CAPTAIN MYLES STANDISH,
the first commissioned military officer of New England.
Laid on the summit of Captain's Hill, in Duxbury,
under the superintendence of the
Ancient and Honorable Artillery Company
of Massachusetts,
in presence of
THE STANDISH MONUMENT ASSOCIATION,
by the
M. W. Grand Lodge of Free Masons of Massachusetts,
M. W. Sereno D. Nickerson, Grand Master,
on the Seventh Day of October, A. D. 1872,
Being the two hundred and fifty-second year since
the first settlement of New England
by the
PILGRIM FATHERS.

—

Site consecrated August 17, 1871.
Association incorporated May 4, 1872.
Association organized and ground broken June 17, 1872.
Corner of foundation laid August 9, 1872.

The Grand Master, after an examination of the stone, declared it square; the box was placed and wedged in position; the block was consecrated with corn, wine, and oil, and duly laid by the Grand Master according to the form prescribed in the Masonic Ritual; the blessing of God was invoked upon the workmen, and the desire expressed that the monument should perpetuate the memory of the pioneer leader whose remembrance it was intended to promote.

There were from eight to ten thousand people present. During the exercises Brown's Band performed a solemn invocation, and the soloists gave the trumpet calls, and Baxter's Battery fired a salute.

The exercises were observed with great interest by the multitude present; and at their conclusion, the celebrants adjourned from labor to refreshment, the Association and the Masons being provided for by the ladies of Duxbury, and the Military by Mr. J. B. Smith, the celebrated caterer.

DINNER OF THE ANCIENTS.

At 3 o'clock the Ancient and Honorable Artillery Company proceeded to the tent, under which an excellent dinner was spread by J. B. Smith. Four hundred plates were laid, and they were all occupied. The Divine blessing was invoked by Rev. Dr. George E. Ellis, of Boston, after which half an hour was devoted to a discussion of the ample and elegant repast provided by the caterer. This being accomplished, Capt. Wyman called his command to order, and addressed them as follows: —

Speech of Capt. Wyman.

Gentlemen of the Ancient and Honorable Artillery Company: — Through the kind invitation of the Standish Monument Association, we are here to-day to join with them in laying the corner-stone of a monument that shall commemorate the valor and sagacity of the first military commander of Massachusetts — Captain Myles Standish. Our hero seems to have been born and bred for the very position he was to occupy. In early life he was trained to the hardships and trials of war, having been commissioned at the age of twenty, a lieutenant in the army, serving in the Low Countries against the armies of the Inquisition. During the years 1619 and 1620, we find him with the refugees, at Leyden, and joining with them in their expedition to the New World. His military education and ability were at once recognized, and he was made the first military commander of the Plymouth Colony. His courage knew no bounds; he was ready to meet danger in any form. He was often sent on expeditions to reduce white men, as well as Indians, to subjection. His mode of warfare was effective and decisive. It is appropriate that the first military commander of the colony from which Massachusetts and New England sprung should be recognized. The people of his own day appreciated his great ability, both as a soldier and a civilian, and looked to him for protection from the hostile tribes that surrounded them and for the enforcement of laws and the preservation of order. It was his strong arm and his great courage that enabled our fathers to maintain their existence as a colony, and transmit to us the glorious heritage we now enjoy. They manifested their appreciation of his deeds of valor and of civil service, by presenting him with the farm upon which we have to-day laid the corner-stone of a monument to his memory; a monument that shall perpetuate the remembrance of their gift and the recognition of those living two hundred and fifty years after, that Captain Myles Standish was the man to whom we are more indebted than any other for the preservation of the infant colony. We rear this monument to his memory on the spot where he and the noble men with whom he acted have no doubt stood and looked out upon the beautiful landscape and the glorious sea, and exclaimed, as we have in our hearts to-day, "The lines are fallen unto us in pleasant places. Yea, we have a goodly heritage." The fields over which we have marched were made consecrated ground by the footsteps of the grand old Pilgrims. Here lived and labored Standish and Elder Brewster. I stand with one foot on the farm of Elder Brewster, and one on the farm of Myles Standish. Could they and their compeers be with us to-day, what would be their astonishment at the mighty changes that have been wrought? Could they have come with us this morning from our metropolis, which was then only an outskirt of their colony, over the iron road, in an hour and a half, a distance which in their time would have been a two days' journey, and have marched with us to the heights above, they would see —

> "Where peeped the hut, the palace towers,
> Where skimmed the bark the war-ship lowers;
> Joy gayly carols where was silence rude,
> And cultured thousands throng the solitude."

I will not longer occupy your time, for I see around me gentlemen in whose veins courses the Pilgrim blood, who will eloquently tell you of the grandeur, devotion, and heroism of the Fathers.

The after proceedings were entirely informal, each speaker being introduced in a few pleasant words. Dr. Ellis was the first gentleman called up, as one well versed in the history of the colony and of New England.

Speech of the Rev. George E. Ellis, D. D.

Mr. Commander and Gentlemen: — It is to be taken for granted that the large majority — if not all — of those who sit around these crowded tables, and have shared in the previous observances of this day, know enough of our local ancestral history, and of the household traditions kept alive amid these homes by those who remain in them and who have gone from them, to feel the full spirit of this occasion. The famous Pilgrim Soldier, for whose enduring memorial the solid column of granite is to rise over the corner-stone just firmly planted on its bed, is the genius of this spot. If there be any here who are ignorant of his personality, his service, and his right to such a memorial, they must have found and felt a quickening impulse to acquaint themselves with his history, from the inspiration of what they have already seen and heard to-day. We stood together, in this fine autumn air, upon that bold, rounded promontory, so distinctly lifted out of this undulating region around it, and so grandly overlooking the bay and the shore redolent with all the blessed memories of the Pilgrims. Down near the water's edge at the left hand, east of this tent, is the site of the dwelling of Myles Standish, from whence he looked up to this hill, given to him in gratitude for service.

From his homestead, when occasion called him to the village settlement at Plymouth, it was easier for him to take to the water in his skiff, two miles, than to follow the footpath of the thickets, of eight miles. He must often have mounted this hill-top of his domain, and enjoyed the grand and pleasant spectacle that opened before him at the east. He could look upon all the features and objects of this remarkable harbor with which he had become familiar before a final landing had been made by his company. For we call to mind that five weeks elapsed after the day when the Mayflower anchored in the bay and the famous Compact was signed in its cabin, before that company planted itself on the soil. The historic landing day, which is commemorated, is dated one week earlier on Monday, completing four weeks after their arrival. But this was made by only a portion of the company, in the third of the exploring expeditions so laboriously pursued by them all around this spot in their shallop. For amid all their straits, after long and wearing confinement and sea-fare on board their crowded vessel, and in spite of the anxiety of the captain to be rid of them lest his own provisions for the homeward voyage should fail, they used much deliberation in their choice. In all three of these expeditions, it would appear that Myles Standish was the right arm of their reliance for all terrestrial needs, while Elder Brewster remained with the major portion of the company on board the anchored vessel to supplicate almost hourly the divine direction. On the Sunday previous to the day of historic commemoration, the exploring party under Standish had landed from their shallop and kept the Sabbath on that pleasant little sheltered island which we have seen from the hill-top, and which they named after their pilot, Clarke. We remember, too, that on this third expedition, the explorers having landed for the night on the shore of the bay of Wellfleet, had there first called into use the military prowess of their Captain. Roused by their sentinels at midnight, they were set upon by an unknown company of savages, and his bullets were of avail without his sword to drive them off before they had done further harm. The spot was appropriately named by the wanderers "First Encounter." On this same expedition they were much pleased with the spot behind us, where the river, to which they gave the name of their captain, "Jones," empties into the bay. They would, indeed, have made their settlement there, within the present bounds of Kingston, had it not been so deep in the bay and with an insufficient harbor. They could hardly have failed to mark the beauty, the capacity, and safety of this harbor, as they traced out its protection from wintry gales by that remarkable promontory which, starting from the shore of Marshfield, runs out like a miniature Italy, sweeping a course of seven miles, and terminates a heel and toe with the points of the Gurnet and Saquish.

We know but little of the personal history of this valiant champion of the Pilgrims, — nothing, indeed, until we find him, seemingly by mere chance, joining himself to the company of some of their leading spirits during their sojourn at Leyden. His own name, and the name given to this township of Duxbury, where his estate lay, identify him with a family and manor of high consideration in Lancashire, Old England. And Morton, the secretary of the Old Colony, says he was of that family, and was defrauded of his rights as heir apparent. When his parents gave him in baptism the name Myles, — the old Roman word for soldier, — they little knew how effectively he would vindicate his fitness to bear it. Serving as an English soldier in the Low Countries, he there made his first acquaintance with some of Robinson's congregation at Leyden, and it was either at their solicitation or by his own prompting, that he joined them in their enterprise hither. Not knowing the date of his birth, we do not know to what age he had arrived when he died here in 1656. But thirty-six years of severe and exhausting service, on hard and scanty fare, with painful, wearying, and dangerous expeditions, which make up his record here, are to be added to whatever may have been the length of his previous life. We may try to think of him as having attained the full age of man, with a brief interval of leisure and repose as a farmer on these acres before he found his full rest.

The most curious fact in his personal history in his connection with the Pilgrim company, considering how close and warm were the relations of confidence and dependence between him and them, was, that he was only what we may call a "proselyte of the gate." Though he seems to have been a regular worshipper with the congregation, and a devout, or at least an acquiescent, participant in all the occasions of fasting and thanksgiving, and in all religious exercises of morning and evening prayer, grace at meals, and of "waiting on the Lord" in every enterprise and expedition, yet he never joined himself to them in church communion. He was not a man of "professions"; nor, so far as we know, of "confessions." He was never "sealed," or "covenanted." We are at a loss for the explanation of this fact, considering the standard and the expectations of his associates. Was there some such obvious and lamentable lack of "grace" in him that the brethren and sisters would have hesitated to allow him to pass the ordeal, if he had risked it? Or was he withheld from subjecting himself to it by true humility, a consciousness of the old Adam unsubdued in him, as one given to carnal weapons? We know that he was an irritable and passionate man, and that his quick temper was easily stirred and then not curbed. Possibly, too, when in these moods, or under provocation, he may have allowed himself a free use of some emphatic words in the vernacular which do not become the lips of saints. He was a little man, of short stature. And being of so hot a spirit, it is to his credit that we read that he controlled himself for the moment when taunted for his small size by those Indian ruffians, Wituwamat and Pecksuot, two of the conspirators whose plots he so summarily thwarted by killing them at Weston's plantation at Weymouth.

But if the Old Colony captain was a man rather of works than of faith, those of us here who come from the sister Colony of the Bay have no occasion to boast ourselves on the score of our champion at the time, who held a corresponding position there in military rank. Captain John Underhill was indeed a very black sheep, one of the sorriest of saints, and a grievous scandal to the Boston church of which he was one of the earliest members. It was found much more difficult to get him out of it than it had been to draw him into it, though the pure-minded Winthrop and the rest of the brethren valued his qualities as a bold soldier. He was an Antinomian not only in sturdy avowal, but also in scandalous doings which here cannot be rehearsed. He was so sure, while quietly enjoying his pipe, that he had received the seal of the Spirit in inward sanctification, that he could venture to be even reckless and to follow his bent in the matter of "works." He said, on being convented before the church for gross offences, that "the Spirit had sent into him a full assurance of free grace, while he was in the moderate enjoyment of the creature called tobacco." Of the two captains, in the early Indian warfare, and in the straits of dangerous enterprise, the uncovenanted Standish is to be preferred. It may be a matter of surprise with some that Standish never attained any higher military rank and title than that of captain. We can answer only that he held the highest military office which the colony had to bestow, and that he had no rival, no superior, no peer. There were not men enough at the time to give him the title over a larger military organization, and the women of the time had not sought to extend their sphere by enrolment. Some of these, however, though not in the ranks, did good service on occasion from out of loop-holes in their dwellings, and behind hay-ricks. Standish's command was in a year after the settlement divided into four companies, with proper subordinate offices. He was, in a fitting and high sense of the term, a providential man, and he well deserved the honors and the memorial here bestowed.

Speech of Mr. Charles Deane.

(Mr. Charles Deane, of Cambridge, rose in response to a sentiment in allusion to " the editor of Governor Bradford's long-lost History of Plymouth Plantation," published a few years ago by the Massachusetts Historical Society; and said, —)

I could not resist the temptation, Mr. Commander, to accept your kind invitation to come down here to-day, and to share with you the pleasure of standing for the first time on " Captain's Hill," near which the ashes of our old hero repose; and though I do not rise to make a formal speech, it would certainly be very ungracious in me not to respond to your request to say a single word. It is eminently fit that the Ancient and Honorable Artillery Company should join in the ceremonies of this occasion in doing honor to the memory of the famous captain of the Pilgrim band. I would not draw any invidious comparisons between a number of noble men, each of whom performed the highest service in laying the foundations of the Pilgrim colony, — the *seed-plot* of New England, I could almost say of the nation. They all claim our highest regard. There was Bradford, in civil capacity the Washington of the colony, its governor for thirty years, and its principal historian, to whose memory in a fitting time a suitable monument should be erected. Then there was Elder Brewster, for many years the only preacher in the colony. There was Governor Winslow, a most accomplished man, fit to stand before kings. I will not enumerate others. But Captain Standish, the commander of the ancient and honorable military force of the Plymouth colony, has eminent claims to your notice. Of what avail, sir, would have been the compact on board the Mayflower? of what avail the civil polity of fundamentals framed a few years later? (for the colony had no royal charter of incorporation, and was self-governing throughout), — of what use, I say, would have been all these civil functions, if the colony had not material strength to endure: force enough to defend itself against the savages who sought its life? Many of the Indians proved friendly to the last; but a few were deadly hostile, and some terrible examples had to be made, and Standish was the instrument of execution. No sooner had the colony begun to recover from the shock of the dreadful sickness and mortality of the first winter, when one half their number was swept away, than an efficient organization was made of the military force of the community. Standish was chosen commander, and he organized his little company by dividing it into four squadrons, assigning quarters to each to which they were to repair in case of sudden alarm.

You have referred, sir, to Governor Bradford's History of the colony. No one can read that old authentic chronicle without realizing the importance of the services rendered by Captain Standish during a long period in the history of the settlement, both as civil magistrate and military commander. He had served in the Low Countries, and had a thorough knowledge of military tactics. He had joined the Pilgrims in Holland, and fortunate it was for them that he embarked with the Mayflower company. The events of the last few years have called attention to the importance of the military arm in time of danger. "The cankers of a calm world and a long peace" were, I fear, leading us to lose sight of this. Captain Standish proved himself equal to every emergency, if we except that of winning the smiles of Priscilla Mullins, in which traditionary adventure John Alden, the young cooper, unwittingly carried off the prize. This little episode has been wrought into a beautiful poem by Mr. Longfellow, who, with a license which poets always claim, has invested it with incidents which our sober chronicles have failed to record. In the distant future these charming fictions, like the stories of the old bards of Britain, will be recited for veritable history.

Not unlike many great military commanders, Captain Standish

was a small man in size, and it is said that the grace of patience was not his. An old contemporary writer says of him: "A little chimney is soon fired: so was the Plymouth captain, a man of very small stature, yet of a very hot and angry temper." The saintly Robinson, of Leyden, on hearing of the execution which Standish had done upon a number of hostile Indians at Wessagusset (now Weymouth), in 1623, wrote thus to Governor Bradford: "How happy a thing had it been if you had converted some before you had killed any. . . . Upon this occasion let me be bold to exhort you seriously to consider the disposition of your captain, whom I love, and am persuaded the Lord, in great mercy and for much good, hath sent to you, if you use him aright." I dare say the captain would have replied to such warning, that there was little opportunity, in the terrible exigency of that occasion, for enforcing the mild lessons of the Christian code upon those demons in human shape. Cromwell's motto was, "Trust in the Lord, and keep your powder dry." How far Standish may have cherished the "trust" commended in this maxim we are not distinctly told. He was not a member of the Plymouth church, and there are strong suspicions that the doctrine of the perseverance of the saints had not taken strong hold of him. But we know he always kept his powder dry and his weapons bright; and on all occasions his conduct was strictly defensible on the rules of duty imposed upon him as the military leader of the colony.

An interesting picture of Plymouth, in which a glimpse of our captain appears, is given in a letter written by a Dutchman, De Rasieres, of Manhattan, who visited the colony in 1627 for purposes of trade, — coming up through Buzzard's Bay and crossing over from Manomet. After describing the place, its houses and gardens, he proceeds: "Upon the hill they have a large square house with a flat roof, made of thick sawn plank, stayed with oak beams; upon the top of which they have six cannon which shoot iron balls of four and five pounds weight, and command the surrounding country. [This was built in 1622.] The lower part they use for their church, where they preach on Sundays and the usual holidays. They assemble by beat of drum, each with his musket or firelock, in front of the captain's door. They have their cloaks on, and place themselves in order, three abreast, and are led by a sergeant, without beat of drum. Behind comes the governor in a long robe. Beside him, on the right hand, comes the preacher, with his cloak on; and on the left hand the captain, with his side arms and his cloak on and with a small cane in his hand, — and so they march in good order, and each sets his arms down near him."

That is the way they went to church in Plymouth in 1627. The governor, with his long robe, was Bradford; the preacher, on his right hand, was Elder Brewster; the captain, with his side arms, was Myles Standish.

But, Mr. Commander, I have already occupied too much of your precious time, and will now give way to others who are to address you. [Applause.]

Remarks of Gen. Sargent.

Capt. Wyman introduced General Sargent in an exceedingly complimentary manner, saying that they had heard much of the courage of Myles Standish, but that they had now the pleasure of welcoming a gentleman who had proven himself not a whit less brave.

Gen. Sargent responded as follows: "Thanking you, sir, for a compliment which somewhat abashes me, from a painful consciousness of its disproportion to any small merit of mine; I thank you also for the honor of your invitation and the cordiality of your welcome. I am truly glad to meet the members of an organization which has preserved from early days the traditions of respect for soldierly service. I agree with the remarks made by that great soldier, Irvin McDowell, at a recent dinner of the Society of the Army of the Potomac, that, until the Millennium shall really come, the need of an arm-bearing, fighting force behind the laws must continue and be felt. No appeal to the courtesy of ruffians and lawbreakers will be so effective to preserve the peace of society, as to justify us in dispensing with a trained and disciplined military power. The grave exigencies of society cannot be trifled with. Mobs cannot be dispersed by sighs of aspiration. I trust that I shall be forgiven by the ladies present, when I say that I do not see in female suffrage a panacea for social disorders: — nay, in a composite government like ours, where states may come into conflict with other states, or with the national government, I think that any proposition to create a numerical show of voting majorities, which the real, physical, enforcing majorities do not back up and support, is a subject of alarm. The ballot is the proper privilege of manhood, because the ballot, without a musket behind it, is a delusion and a snare. If I am answered that women have proved that they can fight upon the battle-field, I say, God forbid that womanly nature, as men love it, should be dragged through the fury and crime and blood of carnage, such as soldiers know it to be. Women, as God made them, are too pure and holy to be thought of in such brutalizing associations. If I am answered again, that women may support their votes as well as men, by camp service and giving their personal assistance to wounded and in hospitals, I am forced to a little arithmetical calculation. The number of the sexes is about equal. If women shall vote and take their part in the duties of the camp, there would be a hundred thousand nurses, — a large number to take care of the ten or twenty thousand men who might be wounded in a battle where a hundred thousand men of the same side might be engaged. The condition of things in this case reminds me of a pretty picture published in "Harper's Weekly" during the war. The scene was a hospital. An elegantly dressed, well bonneted, beautifully gloved young lady was leaning over a couch, where a pale and haggard, but handsome soldier lay. There were other cots in the ward with soldiers on them as ugly as the artist's chalk and charcoal could make them. He had not painted any beautiful young women at their bedsides. "Can I do anything for you to-day, my poor fellow?" said the angel. "No, ma'am, I feel very sick." — "O, I must do something; can't I fan you?" "O, no, ma'am! I'm as cold as ice." — "Shan't I read to you?" "O, no, ma'am! my head aches."—"Well, let me sponge your face for you, and then I'll go."—"O, no, ma'am!"—"O! do let me!"—"Well, ma'am, if you're set upon it, you may; but you're the thirty-fifth blessed woman that's done it this morning."

Far be it from me to say one word that may be in the least construed as a disrespect to the just and proper claims of the better part of humanity to the fullest recognition, the highest remuneration, and the most respectful honors in every field of intellectual, moral, and physical employment that does not degrade womanhood. But, before an assembly of citizen soldiers, I should be false to myself if I did not express my conviction that the duties of the ballot-box and of the cartridge-box are inseparable, and may not properly be devolved upon those beings who seem placed between man and the higher powers as the medium of his holier inspiration.

With the hope, gentlemen, that through the future of American history, the military spirit may be transmitted from one generation of citizen soldiers to another, and with my cordial thanks for your courtesy, I close my somewhat too extended remarks."

The following letter was received from the President of the United States, and its reading during the exercises was greeted with three hearty cheers: —

EXECUTIVE MANSION,
WASHINGTON, D. C., Sept. 30, 1872.

Dear Sir, — I have the honor to acknowledge the receipt of your very polite invitation to be present at the laying of the corner-stone of the Standish Monument on the 7th of October, and beg you to accept for yourself and on behalf of the association, my sincere thanks for the kind attention. It would afford me much pleasure to be able to contribute by my presence to the commemoration of one whose memory is held in such grateful regard as America's Pilgrim soldier, but my official duties will detain me in Washington.

Very respectfully your obedient servant,

U. S. GRANT.

STEPHEN M. ALLEN, Esq.,
Cor. Sec'y Standish Monument Association.

Other letters received from Generals Sherman, Sheridan, and Dix, were read and properly responded to.

Gov. Padelford, of Rhode Island, being called out, made a few felicitous remarks, during which he said that he felt honored when upon the soil of Massachusetts, a State full of military power and spirit, and which had the first regiment at Washington in the late rebellion. It was but a short time since that he had the pleasure of welcoming the Ancients to the State of Rhode Island, and the feelings he then expressed were shared in by all the military organizations of Providence.

He was followed by Adjutant-General Cunningham, of Massachusetts, Adjutant-General Moran, of Rhode Island, and Colonel Edward W. Kinsley, who each made brief speeches, which were fully appreciated.

Major Charles W. Stevens then read the following original lines, which were well received by all present: —

Can you really, dear Captain, invite my poor pen,
On occasion like this, when the wisest of men,
Have caught from each billow that breaks on the shore,
Some sweet inspiration of days gone before?

When the songs of the poet and poetess sweet,
Have hallowed each grass blade that lies at our feet;
Rehearsed in its pathos, its pride, and its glory
The Mayflower's voyage and the Puritan's story?

That I, though an "Ancient," should dare to remember
The perils and hardships of that drear December;
How much less to recount in feeblest of rhyme,
The noble devotion, the action sublime,

Of him, brave defender of weak and of strong,
Who, striking for right, always conquered the wrong;
Myles Standish the hero, the captain, the sage,
Whose name 's high enrolled upon History's page;

To-day, near the spot where they laid him to rest,
By the sea-beaten shore and the wave's breaking crest,
Right gladly we come to the land of our birth
To rear the tall shaft that shall honor his worth.

'T is fitting and right that the oldest command
Throughout the whole length and the breadth of the land,
To the oldest of captains should homage pay,
By accepting this trust on their fall field-day.

That we 've long loved brave Myles, and to-day better still,
Is shown by the ranks that have marched up his hill,
For far greater merit might tempt us in vain
To venture once more such a fearful campaign.

It's a fact, — keep it shady, don't mention it here, —
That to strengthen their courage they spoke of the cheer
Which awaited their coming, and whispered once more
Of the savory clam on the Duxbury shore.

Could those stern, rock-bound Pilgrims come back to us now,
And climb once again this old hill to its brow,
How would their grave faces in glad surprise stare
As they gazed on these tables of Puritan fare!

How proudly our fortitude, courage, and zeal
Would they loudly applaud, reverentially feel,
Could they know the privations, the suff'ring, and toil
Each "Ancient" endured setting foot on this soil!

Could they still farther go, and our daily lives view,
How we shun wealth and honor for all that is true;
How we court obscurity, poverty, loss,
And count the world's splendors nothing but dross; —

Exulting with reverend emotions of pride,
They would feel not in vain had they suffered and died
That the lessons they taught of frugality, thrift,
So firmly were anchored they never could drift.

And those stanch Pilgrim mothers, Priscilla and Rose,
Whom our daughters take after and fashion their clothes;
They would view with delight with what vigor and skill
Their fond papa's purses they labor to fill.

How above all else in this life they enjoy,
In kitchen and nursery their time to employ;
That in marriage relations they tighten the cords,
And bow to the will of their Puritan lords.

I notice, Commander, you quietly smile,
As if your poor muse were sarcastic the while;
But if you least doubt that she sings not in tune,
Take breakfast with me the "first Monday in June."

And then — well, skip that, the question now
Is, How shall your muse make her best parting bow?
Why not? — yes I have it — the most proper way, —
A toast to the soldier we honor to-day.

The Puritan Captain, Myles Standish the brave,
Though he sleeps, alas, in a nameless grave,
His virtues revered shall outlive in their fame
The proud column you rear to honor his name.

Speech of Major Ben: Perley Poore.

Mr. Commander: — However hostile the savage residents on Indian Hill may have been, I can assure you that those who now dwell there are peaceful admirers of the plucky little captain so deservedly honored here to-day. We who reside in what was the Colony of Massachusetts Bay, have not forgotten how he came over to Gloucester in 1625, and got in a furious rage, which nearly produced bloodshed, about a fishing-stage which some Plymouth men had set up the year previous, and which others had occupied after they went home. Good Roger Conant made peace, and so instead of reckoning Myles Standish among our enemies, we can regard him as we regard no other Plymouth colonist who figures in history, with unqualified veneration and admiration. Bigoted, austere, and intolerant, the leading Puritans established a block ade against the pleasant sports and games of "merrie England," and "attempted to make the colony, as it were, a convent of Puritan devotees, — except in the allowance of marriage and money-making, — subjected to all the rules of the stricter monastic orders." Fortunately, Captain Standish, who was with them, but not of them, seasoned this arrogant intolerance with the jovial spice of camp life, and more fortunate for us was it that these zealots were forced (as we have seen their successors in our day) to call upon the man of the sword in their hour of need, and to tolerate his freedom of action, while they submitted to his drill and discipline. Thus did one brave little captain leaven the whole lump of Plymouth Puritans.

I have often regretted, Mr. Commander, that Captain Standish could not have been permitted to belong to the Ancient and Honorable Artillery Company which you now so acceptably lead, as was that equally brave Indian fighter of Essex county, Daniel Denison. There was a company chartered there also, Mr. Commander, in 1638, "for the advancement of the military art and the advancement of arms," but in 1653 its captain was invited to remove from Ipswich to Boston to succeed Sedgwick as Major-General of the Province, and it gradually became absorbed in this company, which, in 1660, perfected the alliance by electing General

Denison as its commander. Since then, the men of Essex have always been found in the ranks of the Ancients; they have enjoyed its honors, and they have furnished a goodly number of its chaplains.

We, Mr. Commander, have reason to feel proud that in this time-honored corps, the martial fires lighted by Captain Standish have ever been sacredly fed with patriotism and kept burning, even when public opinion, inheriting Puritan intolerance, has enlisted the weapons of argument, ridicule, and misrepresentation against military organizations and military men. As it has been in the past, so may it be in the future. Whenever the war-drums beat to arms, may the Ancients be ready to stand by their country's flag, and stalwartly defend it against domestic assailants and foreign foes. And when the silver trumpets of peace are heard in the land, may the Ancients be equally ready to parade with full ranks as to-day, to honor the memory of the departed brave, to revive old friendships, and to enjoy clam-bakes. Men will die, — but let the martial, tolerant, jovial spirit of Myles Standish be perpetuated forever.

The Commander having introduced the Grand Master of Masons in Massachusetts, Mr. Nickerson responded as follows: —

Mr. Commander: — It seems eminently fit and proper that the ceremonies of an occasion intended to do honor to the first commissioned officer of the New World should be participated in by the oldest military organization on this continent, and by the representatives of the oldest human organization in the world. It is true, sir, that the members of the Fraternity I have the honor to represent, are men of peace. Love of mankind is one of the first lessons we are taught in Masonry. Peace, unity, and harmony are the grand aims we have in view. If all men were Masons, and all lived up to the principles we profess, there would be no work for military organizations. But, unhappily, such is not the case; and therefore, we must continue to preach the gospel of peace, and you and we, if need be, must be ready to fight for it.

Although the two organizations would seem, at first thought, to have nothing in common, yet history shows them to have been often in very close connection, especially in this country.

First among the military men whom we are proud to claim as members of our Fraternity, we reckon him who was "first in war, first in peace, and first in the hearts of his countrymen." On many public as well as private occasions, he wore the regalia of Master of a Lodge, which Madame de Lafayette had presented to him, and which she had wrought with her own hands. For many years after Gen. Washington's death this regalia was sacredly preserved, and never worn by any other person until it was assumed by the Marquis de Lafayette himself, on the occasion of his reception by the Lodge in Alexandria in the year 1824.

It is a fact, which will probably be new to many of you, that during the whole of the Revolutionary War, every general officer was a Mason. It was the special request of General Washington that all of them should be connected with the Fraternity. Furthermore, I believe it to be true that during most of that war nearly all the officers above the rank of captain were members of our Order.

Gen. Joseph Warren, who laid down his life for his country at the battle of Bunker Hill, on the 17th of June, 1775, the very day on which Gen. Washington received his commission as Commander-in-Chief, was at that very time our loved and honored Grand Master.

I may also remind you of the long roll of officers, brethren of the mystic tie, who rendered distinguished services to the country during the war of the rebellion. Of the many Masons numbered among the rank and file, I think it is not too much to say that they were among the best soldiers; a fact which I attribute in a large degree to our principles and our practice in the matter of subordination, obedience to constituted authority and regard for law and order.

To come down to later times, I may instance the fact, that about one half of the brethren who have accompanied me to-day officially are members of the Ancient and Honorable Artillery Company, and we claim about the same proportion of those who have worn your uniform.

I am not aware that Myles Standish was one of the Craft, but he certainly practised in an exemplary manner the four cardinal virtues which are most impressively inculcated as binding upon Masons, — Temperance, Fortitude, Prudence, and Justice. We are not informed that he ever failed in the exercise of these virtues, except in the instance recorded by the poet when he showed the white feather, and confessed, —

"I can march up to a fortress and summon the place to surrender,
But march up to a woman with such a proposal, I dare not.
I'm not afraid of bullets, nor shot from the mouth of a cannon,
But of a thundering, "No!" point-blank from the mouth of a woman,
That I confess I'm afraid of, nor am I ashamed to confess it!"

His success was not such as to encourage others to follow his example, for we are told that the messenger and the maiden made up a match between them, and left the "little Captain" out in the cold. I trust the Ancients will always have the courage to speak for themselves in such cases, although I am obliged to confess that some in my company have thus far been sadly lacking in this kind of fortitude. Myles Standish found this

"a land of sand and sickness and sorrow,
Short allowance of victual and plenty of nothing but gospel!"

We have found abundance of sand, but, thanks to the Ancient and Honorable Artillery Company, no "short allowance of victual." For these pleasures of the table and for the numerous other courtesies you have extended to us to-day, permit me, Mr. Commander, to return our sincere thanks, and to conclude with the hope that, while we shall continue to preach the gospel of peace, the members of both organizations may be found in the future as in the past, to stand shoulder to shoulder ready, if need be, to fight for it.

The Commander stated that he saw around the tables many gentlemen whom he had expected to call upon; but as the hour fixed for the departure for Boston had arrived, and as time and steam wait for no man, he must give the order to "fall in."

On the reverse side of the Plate enclosed in the Corner-Stone, were the names of the Officers of the Association (as named on pages 3 and 4), with the additional superscription as follows: —

ALDEN FRINK, *Architect.* NATH'L ADAMS, *Master of Construction.*

FRANCIS STANDISH and EDWIN ADAMS,
Superintendents of Construction.

JOHN S. LORING, *Engineer.*

ULYSSES S. GRANT, *President of the United States.*
SIDNEY L. PERHAM, *Governor of Maine.*
JOHN W. STUART, *Governor of Vermont*
WILLIAM B. WASHBURN, *Governor of Massachusetts.*
EDWARD A. STRAW, *Governor of New Hampshire.*
MARSHALL JEWELL, *Governor of Connecticut.*
SETH PADELFORD, *Governor of Rhode Island.*

THOMAS CHANDLER, CHARLES H. CHANDLER, SAMUEL ATWELL,
Selectmen of Duxbury.

Myles Standish

KITCHEN OF STANDISH HOUSE.

THE ASSOCIATION DINNER.

A SPLENDID dinner was served to the members of the Monument Association and their invited guests in a mammoth tent, in which some seven hundred plates were laid. The centre supports of the tent were ornamented with bouquets of wild flowers and autumn leaves, and one beautiful wreath of roses and other bright flowers, the contribution of Mrs. Harrison Gray Otis. The word "Standish" was placed on the walls of the tent in evergreen, and neat bouquets, arranged with feminine taste, graced the tables. The guests were seated at the tables about three o'clock.

The exercises were conducted by General Sargent. Prayer was offered by the Rev. Mr. Burgess of Duxbury. After the repast, which was prepared and provided by the ladies of Duxbury, and dispensed from their hands, had been disposed of, the chairman, in behalf of the Association, returned thanks to the ladies for their generous assistance.

SPEECH OF GEN. SARGENT.

Ladies and Gentlemen:—As president of this Association, it is my agreeable duty to welcome you to this collation, which the ladies of Duxbury have so bountifully provided. But if John Alden was embarrassed in making love for another man to one woman, I may shrink a little from the task of expressing to so many my own most respectful sentiments and those of my colleagues in this Association. And yet our charming hostesses, the ladies of Duxbury, are only following the example of that first woman, dear mother Eve, who got herself into a scrape through her kind heart, and her desire to give the first man whom she met something delicious to eat.

It was her kindness of heart, rather than curiosity or vanity or any weak motive, that led her astray. We often accuse the dear creatures, her daughters, of vanity. But men are vainer than women. For they have much more to be vain of. Do not start with horror at my proposition, — but let me prove it. What may a woman expect as the dream and crowning triumph of a life? To marry some man. What is that compared with the glory of the other sex, every one of which may expect to marry a woman and take an angel to his heart and home. And I do not use this term lightly. Is not she who staid the *last* at the cross, is not she who came *first* to the tomb of our Lord, something a little nearer the angel than are men? In fact, when I have viewed that beautiful picture where Mary and Peter the apostle are represented as looking into the sepulchre from which the stone had been rolled away, I have hardly been able to say whether the light upon her features came from the angel sitting within. I have been willing to think, rather, that it was the heavenly light from that sweet, pale face of womanly devotion which shone upon him and filled the tomb with glory.

It is this spirit of devotion to the true, the noble, the self-sacrificing, the good, that has animated, as every soldier knows, the patriotic women of this country, as she has passed through the agony of her glory. It is this spirit that respects the memory of the great pilgrim soldier, and welcomes with hospitable hands those who honor him to-day. If he required any leaf of laurel for his fame, the grateful recognitions of his service by the fair descendants of the Pilgrims to-day, on the very spot of his dwelling place, after two centuries have established his title to our gratitude — would supply it. Ladies, in his name, and in the name of the Association created to do him honor, we thank you for your gracious and grateful hospitality.

The following telegram from General Ulysses S. Grant, President of the United States, was read, and received by the audience standing: —

"WASHINGTON, D. C., Oct. 7, 1872.

STEPHEN M. ALLEN, *Corresponding Secretary Myles Standish Monument Association, South Duxbury, Mass:* —

I regret my inability to be present to-day at the laying of the corner-stone of the monument to the patriot and soldier, Myles Standish. His name will be green in the history of New-England's great men long after the monument you are about to erect has crumbled into dust.

U. S. Grant."

The first sentiment offered was, "The President of the United States;" to which Hon. Edward S. Tobey responded.

Speech of Hon. E. S. Tobey.

Mr. President: — When I observed the United States revenue cutter at anchor in the Bay at the base of this hill, and heard her national salute, I presumed that the collector of Boston was here, whose prerogative it is to respond to a sentiment in honor of the president of the United States. I regret, for your sake, that you are deprived of the opportunity of listening to his usual appropriate speech and eloquence. But in his absence, I confess that I do not regret the occasion which it affords me to speak in behalf of the great military chieftain of this age, for whose invaluable service to the country the people, with a promptness never equalled, have testified their gratitude by conferring on him the highest honor within their gift. He has, in the telegraphic communication just received, expressed his deep interest in this memorial service, doubtless more fully than, from his well-known habit of reticence, he would have done if personally present. President Grant has made his speeches through his heroic deeds, when at the head of the Union army he led it on to victory, and earned the gratitude of a nation. If the founders of the republic could commit to their great military leader, Myles Standish, so much of magisterial and civil power, may not the people, after the evidence of patriotism, integrity, and executive ability of one of the greatest military leaders of modern times, safely confide still longer in his administration of civil government. Pardon me, if a moment longer shall be occupied in recognition of other relations which I hold to these memorial services. In behalf of the Pilgrim Society, I feel warranted in assuring you of its cordial sympathy with this historic occasion and its worthy object. Under its auspices, a monument, as you are aware, has been completed on the rock in Plymouth, where the Pilgrim Fathers laid the corner-stone of a Christian commonwealth. The foundations of another monument have been also laid in that town on a more elevated and conspicuous site. National in its object, it awaits the general co operation of the people of the United States to complete the superstructure, surmounted by its proposed colossal statue of Faith, with its uplifted arm and finger ever pointing heavenward. And still another monument, not made by human hands, is on yonder beautiful island, where a band of the Pilgrims spent their first Sabbath, with only the blue canopy of heaven to cover them. The Hon. Robert C. Winthrop, in his eloquent oration on Plymouth, on the 250th anniversary of the landing of the Pilgrims, suggested that a monument should be placed on Clark's Island in commemoration of this sublime fact in the history of the Pilgrims. It was my privilege, with other gentlemen, to accompany him and Collector Russell, who kindly detailed the United States revenue cutter for the service, about a year since, to Clark's Island, where a large rock near the centre of the Island was selected as a more appropriate and enduring monument than any artificial structure that could be reared. On its surface, fronting the east, and rising about twenty feet from its base, has been deeply chiselled the terse and characteristic record of the Pilgrims:—

"On the Sabbath day wee rested."

Its foundation, perhaps, lies deeper than even the foundations of the one to be erected here. These monuments shall ultimately crumble into dust; but the monument whose corner-stone was laid on Plymouth Rock, in the principles there announced, shall endure. Be it our duty and that of their descendants, by tradition, by written history, and more than all, by a worthy example, to perpetuate those principles to the end of time.

The sentiment in honor of the "Commonwealth of Massachusetts," was responded to by Dr. Ira L. Moore, a member of the House of Representatives, who alluded to the passage of the act to incorporate the Standish Monument Association, and the efforts he put forth in aid of the measure, as acts which he looked back upon with pride. He believed it would be carried to a full completion, and stand for ages a deserved honor to the brave soldier it commemorates; and in words like the following, referred to Massachusetts: —

" Massachusetts has ever honored the brave. She has always appreciated the sterling integrity and the untiring exertions of her pioneers in establishing her nationality, and the institutions we to-day enjoy. Her coat-of-arms indicates the characteristics of her first settlers in more respects than one. Her conflicts were to " build up " instead of " to destroy." Civilization was to take the place of barbarism, and in no case was it her principle or policy to force with arms what persistent Christian examples and teachings could secure.

" She has honored the Pilgrim settlers on this Bay, and the character of Myles Standish ever has been, and ever will be, dear to our good old Commonwealth. His character was one of action as well as of principle, and discipline was an acknowledged prompting with the government. He upheld and obeyed the laws, and thus his citizenship became valuable, not only to the government of his own day, but to that of our time. We may well pattern by his example and respect his character. I have no doubt the State of Massachusetts will ever hold his memory dear, and cherish his virtues as bright examples for patriotism and honor."

To say that I have felt and still feel a deep interest in the erection of the Myles Standish Monument, is only too true; not only that we may do strict, though *tardy* justice to the memory of one of the most distinguished of that little band of Pilgrims, who were beset with deadly and implacable foes, both from within and without, and by the strength of whose own right arm, in the hands of an overruling Providence, he preserved that little band from utter annihilation.

It became my duty as one of the representatives of Massachusetts, and as one of the committee on mercantile affairs, to examine into and report the charter of the Myles Standish Monument Association, and to defend it upon the floor of the House. If I have been instrumental, as you say, Mr. President, in assisting in procuring the charter, I have done only what I considered it to be my duty.

May the plain granite shaft, the corner-stone of which has been so successfully laid this day, in the presence of the lineal descendants and admiring friends of Myles Standish, continue to rise in its primitive grandeur, until the capstone is reached, upon which shall be placed a bronze statue of the first great Puritan Captain, whose brow shall first be crowned by the earliest rays of the morning sunlight, and the last rays of evening shall gild it with a halo which shall quicken the pulse and revive the hope of the tempest-tossed and shipwrecked mariner, when it shall greet his vision for the first time on arriving in his native land.

But the name and the fame of Myles Standish shall be revered and honored by all true lovers of civil and religious liberty, long after the bronze and the granite, which is to perpetuate his name and fame, shall have mouldered and crumbled into its original dust, by time's effacing fingers.

"The Commonwealth of Rhode Island" was announced with three cheers, and Gov. Padelford responded in a speech filled with historical allusions and patriotic sentiment.

Gen. Sargent then called the Hon. E. S. Tobey to the chair, and ex-Mayor Shurtleff was called upon to respond for the "City of Boston."

Speech of Hon. Nathaniel B. Shurtleff.

Mr. President, Ladies and Gentlemen: — The citizens of Boston will feel pleased that they have been remembered on this pleasant occasion: for the dutiful act which you have in earnest commenced to-day. by laying on Captain's Hill the corner-stone of an enduring memorial, in commemoration of the Pilgrim's Captain, is one that meets the warmest response of sympathy from them, many of whom trace with pride their descent from the worthy forefathers of Pilgrim Land; and whatever is done to hallow the memory of these excellent men, is regarded as highly with us of Boston, as by those who dwell more immediately on the soil which they once trod and cultivated. For, indeed, we have received as much from them, and have been equally benefited by their precepts and example as have you, although like you we do not enjoy the privilege of occupying the places around the hearthstones which they once made happy and prosperous. If the chief magistrate of Boston were here, he would, I assure you, respond most cordially to your sentiment with appropriate remarks; and I know that he will authorize me to thank you in behalf of the city, for your sentiment so kindly expressed.

As for myself, Mr. President, I am glad to be with you to-day, not merely as a Bostonian, but also as a descendant of those men and women of blessed memory, who made the first venture to the Old Colony, to these shores and fields of New England, in 1620. Yet I speak to your company to-day with more than ordinary hesitation, because I fear that the good people of Duxbury will get tired of the voice of one who has been with them so frequently of late. And yet the deep interest which I have in Pilgrim matters, can never so far abate as to prevent me from being present when honor is to be paid to the memory of any of the forefathers, whose names and acts are always fresh in my memory, and whose virtues and principles are indelibly fixed in my heart.

The act of this day, in laying the corner-stone of the Standish Memorial, proceeds from the noblest sentiment of grateful hearts. It is the tribute of filial affection, poured out from willing souls. It is the payment of a debt justly due to one who, notwithstanding hardships, deprivations, and dangers, did much to secure to us the religious and political rights we now so freely possess; and tardy though it be, it is not the less merited, nor does it in any degree detract from its significance, that it is now performed two and a half centuries after the immediate benefits were conferred, — for the great and good results will last forever, and children yet unborn will glory in the Pilgrim name, and bless the dauntless and brave Myles Standish, and his associates, who secured to them the privileges they always will be enabled to enjoy. All praise to the gallant captain, and a grateful remembrance of the glorious exploits of his bravery, prowess, and skill, which struck terror into the hearts of the savage foe that threatened our pious ancestors with total destruction!

But, Mr. President, in raising the memorial to the memory of the chieftain, we do not forget his associates in the great pilgrimage to the barren wilds of rugged New England. We cannot forget the Brewsters, the Aldens, the Cushmans, the Sampsons, the Winsors, the Spragues, the Southworths, and the Bradfords, and other worthies who cast their lots in this ancient town. Their names and virtues live in those of their descendants, and their fame in the results which they accomplished. The heritage which they transmitted is good; may it continue yielding good fruit and be true to ancient principles through all coming time.

While we respect the memory of these worthy people, and glory in their good works, we can but have a feeling of deep regard, bordering nearly on veneration, for the places which they hallowed by their daily walks. Their chosen harbor of rest, where they toiled and prayed and rested from labor, is around about us. The brave captain, the venerable elder, the wise rulers and careful advisers dwelt hereabout. Ancient vestiges now designate their early homes most surely. On yonder knoll, marked by a meagre cluster of dwarfish shrubs, once stood the dwelling of the gallant captain, and beneath their shade are still visible the traces of the humble abode of the captain of the Pilgrims. His grave, unmarked by stone or mound, is with the ancient people of Duxbury, in an almost forgotten graveyard, whose traces are less perceptible than those of the house that served for his shelter in life. Let the exact spot of his resting-place be conclusively determined and fixed; and then let some modest stone, as unpretending as was the sturdy pilgrim, mark the place where he and his immediate family were forever laid to rest beneath the green sods of the ancient God's acre, located by the fathers just under the dripping of their primitive little sanctuary. In doing this, you will perform another act as filial and as dutiful as that which has called you here now; and the modern pilgrim, when he visits the early homes of the forefathers, will regard the deed with thankfulness and gratitude.

The spirit, Mr. President, with which this endeavor, that has called us here to-day, has been commenced and is now prosecuted, will surely warrant ultimate success. Stone by stone will be placed by masters' hands upon the pile you have so auspiciously begun rearing; and before another gathering in of the harvest, the sons and daughters of the Pilgrims will rejoice in the accomplishment of this undertaking. God grant that everything may be propitious, and that no accident may happen to cloud our joy or mar the dutiful effort. Let the column rise to completion; as it will be the first object in this old town to greet the sun at its rising, and the last to bid it adieu at its setting, so may it be to the wayfarer and the mariner a sure guide and a constant friend; and may the captain's memorial be a pleasing reminder of the Pilgrim fathers, and a pledge of our intention to follow in their ways, so as to perpetuate the principles which they so truly inculcated by their example.

SPEECH OF COL. ALBERT J WRIGHT, PRESIDENT OF THE MASSACHUSETTS CHARITABLE MECHANIC ASSOCIATION.

Mr. President, Ladies and Gentlemen: — I esteem it a great honor to be permitted to respond to a sentiment complimentary to the Mechanic Association. I am glad to know that the efficient vice-president of our association, Mr. Nathaniel Adams, is one of the active agents engaged in the good work of erecting an appropriate monument to so notable a character as the heroic Myles Standish; whatever he undertakes is sure to be accomplished.

Myles Standish was one of the most valiant defenders of civil and religious liberty. If not himself a shining light in the church, his life and fortune was at the service of his associates in the little colony who made this region famous by their self-sacrificing devotion to the principles and policy which first brought them to this shore. Here, in this neighborhood, were planted the seeds of civilization, of morals and religion, which, watered by the tears, the prayers, and the faith of the Pilgrim settlers, have grown and flourished, have been diffused as a holy leaven through successive generations to be a blessing to our whole country.

In the full enjoyment of the varied blessings which surround us to-day, it is becoming in us to honor and perpetuate the memory of any of the worthies who first peopled these shores. How forcible are we reminded to-day of the beautiful language of Mr. Charles Sprague, one of our most poetical writers of prose, who, in a Fourth of July oration many years ago, exclaimed, —

"Roll back the tide of time: how powerfully to us applies the promise, 'I will give thee the heathen for an inheritance.' Not many generations ago, where you now sit, encircled with all that exalts and embellishes civilized life, the rank thistle nodded in the wind, and the wild fox dug his hole unscared.

"Here lived and loved another race of beings. Beneath the same sun that rolls over your heads, the Indian hunter pursued the panting deer; gazing on the same moon that smiles for you, the Indian lover wooed his dusky mate. Here, the wigwam blaze beamed on the tender and helpless, the council-fire glared on the wise and the daring. Now they dipped their noble limbs in your sedgy lakes, and now they paddled their light canoe along your rocky shore. Here they warred; the echoing hoop, the bloody grapple; the defying death-song, all were here; and, when the tiger strife was over, here curled the smoke of peace. Here, too, they worshipped; and from many a dark bosom went up a pure prayer to the Great Spirit. He had not written his laws for them on the tables of stone, but had traced them on the tables of their hearts.

"The poor child of nature knew not the God of revelation; but the God of the universe he acknowledged in everything around. He beheld him in the star that sank in beauty behind his lowly dwelling; in the sacred orb that flamed on him from his midday throne; in the flower that snapped in the morning breeze; in the lofty pine that had defied a thousand whirlwinds; in the timid warbler that never left his native grove; in the fearless eagle whose untired pinion was wet in clouds; in the worm that crawled at his foot, and in his own matchless form, glowing with a spark of that light, to whose mysterious source he bent in humble, though blind adoration.

"And all this has passed away.

"Across the ocean came a pilgrim barque, bearing the seeds of life and death The former were sown for you, the latter sprang up in the path of the simple native.

"Two hundred years have changed the character of a great continent, and blotted forever from its face a whole, peculiar people. Art has usurped the bowers of nature, and the anointed children of education have been too powerful for the tribes of the ignorant. Here and there a stricken few remain; but how unlike their bold, untamed, untamable progenitors! The Indian, of falcon glance and lion bearing, the theme of the touching ballad, the hero of the pathetic tale, is gone! And his degraded offspring crawl upon the soil where he walked in majesty, to remind us how miserable is man, when the foot of the conqueror is on his neck."

Mr. President: — We must all be filled with emotions peculiar to the place and the occasion. Every fibre of our system tingles with worship and admiration. We invoke the spirits of those we honor, —

"Manes of Carver, Standish, hear!
To keep the rights you gave, we swear;
And 'midst the storms of State prove true,
To God, our Country, and to you!"

The Chairman then made the following remarks, regretting the absence of the poet, Henry W. Longfellow: —

This is not the first monument to Myles Standish. Amidst the classic shades of Cambridge, America's favorite poet has wreathed a chaplet as imperishable as the English language itself. I am glad that he has described the renowned military chieftain as not yielding to a disappointment, one of the keenest which can affect the human heart, but as heroically devoting his powers more zealously than ever, to the guardianship of the property and interests of the colony. There seems to be a poetic justice in the somewhat remarkable fact that, at this distant day, as one of the descendants of John Alden, I am permitted to unite with you in rearing this monument to Standish, and to participate in these interesting ceremonies. I share with you the regret at Mr. Longfellow's necessary absence; but we are fortunate in the presence of another poet, who will now kindly favor us with an original poem.

I have the pleasure of introducing Samuel B. Noyes, Esq.

Mr. Noyes then recited the following original poem: —

MYLES STANDISH'S FIRST MARCH.

"About ten o'clock we came to a deep valley where we discovered a deer and springs of fresh water.

"We were heartily glad, and sat us down and drunk [says Governor Bradford] our New-England water with as much delight as ever we drunk drink in all our lives."

Unshipp'd for repairs was the Shallop, on shore
  The Mayflower securely lay anchored,
When Standish, Bradford, Hopkins, and Tilly, brave four,
  With the twelve, who to stretch their legs hankered,
Armed with musket, sword, corslet, were set on the land,
  And marched, single file, its wilds to explore;
While Standish was captain, naught dreaded that band
  Of sixteen brave men on the desolate shore.

"The breaking waves" on Long Point dashed high,
  The white eagle soared up to the sun,
The "rocking pines" stretched up to the sky,
  The deer leaped before them — it was fun, —
A picnic, — the sensation was exquisitely new;
  The savages peering from bushes and rock, —
And whistling their dog, when they saw they were few,—
  And every man holding his gun "on the cock."

Onward they went; but, who carried the flask,
  Little bottle aqua-vitæ (so history) —
How much it held, and whose was the task
  To guard it, still to us is mystery.
They took it "straight," till a bubbling spring
  Invited them all to sit down
And they took a long drink, — a little thing, —
  But it brought to that water renown.

And coolly they sat on an Indian mound,
  In that moment of history's dawn, — the brink
Of a future we worshipped as past! hallowed ground
  And of the pure fluid they took their first drink.

What cared that party of sixteen men
  How high on the rocks were breaking
The waves of old ocean, in that blest hour, when
  Pure water their fierce thirst was slaking?

The eagle which had soared with the sun had sunk
  To its nest where the white waves foamed;
The deer went unharmed; had it not, like them, drunk
  Pure water found? So onward they roamed,
'Till on the bare forests came a New-England night,
  And they builded a fire, and around it they lay,
Forgetting their Shallop and the Mayflower, — tight,
  Which rocked, anchor-held, in the turbulent bay.

To-day 't is the brave little captain we sing,
  On this hill where he ended his days ;
To-day let the now fertile valleys loud ring
  While his deeds and his valor we praise.
"Little man" but great "captain" was he;
  Not "gifted in prayer," "he waxed valiant in fight";
"Arm of flesh" to the church, — let his monument be
  Here to raise to his glory, our pride and delight.

The Puritan clergy being announced, Rev. Dr. E. B. Webb was called up, and responded substantially as follows: —

Mr. President: — I am glad that you neither called upon me, nor warned me of your purpose beforehand. Because I have had my clams, and my dinner, without the accompaniment of miserable forebodings.

And now that I am up, allow me to say that I do not quite agree with all that has been said on one point. The work of erecting this monument, or rather of laying the corner-stone, is characterized as tardy.

It would have been well at any time since his death, to recognize the important services of the hardy pioneer and patriotic soldier, Myles Standish. But, recalling what we have had to do as a people, it was hardly to be expected that we should have undertaken this work before. There was no particular danger that the memory of his deeds would die out prematurely, and our hands and hearts have been full of urgent work.

When a colony pulls up stakes, and goes into the far West to-day, there is a great deal to do, — immediate, urgent work. The prairie must be ploughed; the seed must be sown; the fences must be built; the house and barn erected; roads made, and a thousand things beside, before they can stop to think of honors for the dead, or monuments to their memory.

As a people, we have had abundance of such work to do. We are not yet done clearing, ploughing, sowing, building. Besides, we have had laws to frame, and institutions to establish and sustain, and history to make, as well as to write. What wonder, therefore, that with our hands filled, and our minds occupied — constantly, intensely occupied — with the present, what wonder that the knightly soldier has been obliged to wait for his monument on Captain's Hill.

As to the clergy, for whom I am called to respond, I think well of them, as of the soldier. As a rule, they were both true and brave.

They had their full share, I think, in the early persecution, in the subsequent enterprise, and in all the faith and works that have made this country what it is.

The Puritan clergy were not much given to build the tombs of their ancestors, and denounce and destroy every living germ and budding promise of the present. They did refuse allegiance to the worn out theories of the past; they did resist the ecclesiastical hierarchy that strove to tyrannize over them. They preferred freedom to forms, and private judgment to human authority. They put the rights of a living conscience above the claims of a political church. At the same time, fairly tried, they will not be found wanting in veneration or gratitude. That fine sentiment which finds expression in monuments, emblems, paintings, and statues, had a place in their hearts. They have been ready to perpetuate the memory of noble souls, and propagate their virtues.

The men who settled along these shores were greately influenced by the ministers whom they called. But they were in the habit of testing preaching, principles, doctrines, and practice, by God's holy word. They believed the Scriptures to be inspired by the Holy Ghost, and hence they sought models and laws, and precepts for the church and for the state, in these records.

And in these respects, as well as in some others, the present generation would not be damaged by following their example.

The success of our country is assured just in proportion as the open Bible, read by the people, and preached by a regenerate and godly clergy, prevails.

Mr. Myles Standish, of New York, responded for the "New England Society" of New York.

Speech of Myles Standish, Esq.

Mr. President, Ladies and Gentlemen: — Not being gifted as a speaker, and inheriting the characteristic of my ancestor, in not being a "Maker of Phrases," I owe you an apology for occupying even so much of the time, as will suffice for me, as briefly as possible, to meet your requirement; especially, sir, when called upon, without previous notice, to respond for the "New England Society of New York," — a society including many of the ablest men of the metropolis, who, I am sure, would hardly be satisfied with any response I could make for them.

But, Mr. President, when I look around on this large company, and recognize so many eminent men of the country, — men who in their varied walks of life are justly famous, and who by their success have added to the renown of our American manhood; when I see the theological, the administrative, the judicial, the literary, the military, the mechanical, and the mercantile elements of the American people so ably represented, and know that they have gathered here, upon this concecrated spot, simply for the purpose of doing honor to the memory of that devoted band, "which in its noble struggle for liberty of conscience landed on yonder shore two hundred and fifty years ago," by rearing a memorial shaft to its captain, who perhaps, more than all others, by his steadfast purpose and unwavering courage, was an instrument in the hands of Providence, for its protection, and the preservation of the germ of this great Republic, — when I see this, then it is, sir, that I feel there must have been something more than the mere fact of a party of "Exiles" crossing the ocean and making a settlement here, — some deeper meaning and significance to that act, — some principle by them established, which, viewed from the distance of to-day, and in the light of the knowledge gained by the growth and expansion of ideas, seems of sufficient importance to be recognized and commemorated. And, sir, the recognition of the great part played by the Pilgrim Fathers in the progress of the world, is not confined to this people alone; but has extended to a host of thinkers abroad, among whom is, notably, the eminent Spanish writer, Emilio Castellar, who says, in speaking of them, "They bore with them in their frail vessel the immortal spirit of a New World, and a new humanity, the gospel of social redemption, the complement and the crown of religious redemption."

And, sir, I am proud that so much of the blood of that "Band" is mingled in my veins; am proud that among my ancestors is numbered the old Pilgrim Captain; and am highly gratified to find, although two centuries and a half have passed away since his voice awoke these solitudes, and the tramp of his "mighty army of eight men" resounded along these shores, that he still lives in the hearts of this great people, and that their grateful appreciation of his character and his deeds is to find expression in the erection of a monumental column, the corner-stone of which has been to-day so appropriately laid.

And here, sir, I would congratulate the Association upon the happy selection of the site of this monument; for what more fitting place to rear a country's tribute? Here, on the spot where he lived, and, it may be, where he is buried; the spot he loved so well as to make it his home; by its position commanding the land and water for miles around, Captain's Hill, standing, as it were, sentinel-like on guard, is typical of the ever watchful "guardians of the colony," and is in itself a national monument to his worth.

From its summit we can trace, far out at sea, past the rocks and over the shoals that skirt this harbor, the course of the advancing "Mayflower," freighted with the destiny of a glorious republic; from it we see the first land touched by Pilgrim feet, "Clark's Island, and where, it being Sabbath day, we rested"; and opposite, across the Bay, we see "Plymouth Rock," the corner-stone of the nation's monument.

This, then, and none other, is the true place where to commemorate the part Myles Standish took in the promulgation of those vital principles of liberty and equality, before God and man, which, as they stand to-day embodied in the constitution of the United States, are but the natural outgrowth, the lineal descendants of that grand old "compact," signed in the cabin of the "Mayflower," November 21st, 1620.

And now, Mr. President, in closing, I would express to you and to the company, in behalf of Captain Myles Standish, as his descendant and namesake, and on behalf of his descendants generally, my high appreciation of the great honor and respect paid him to-day, and to hope that the "laying of the corner-stone may be speedily followed by the placing of the capstone; and when thus completed, that the monument may ever stand as a constant reminder to every true American, that those great principles for which our forefathers suffered and struggled, "must and shall be maintained."

Lemuel Myles Standish, Esq., of Boston, one of the trustees of the Association, writes an interesting letter from Europe (where he is now travelling), describing his visits to the Standish estates of Duxbury Hall, and Standish Hall in Lancashire, Old England, and regretting his absence from these services.

The following is a copy of the telegram over the French cable, from Captain R. C. Mayne, R. N. C. B.: —

"London, Oct. 7, 1872.

Nath'l Adams, Chairman of the Executive Committee of the Standish Monument Association. The board of directors of the French Atlantic Telegraph Company congratulate the committee on the commencement of their testimony to the worth of one of the noblest of the pioneers of their glorious Country. The board feel proud of the connection of the landing place of their cable with the illustrious name of Myles Standish, and the State of Massachusetts."

SPEECH OF MR. R. T. BROWN, OF THE FRENCH CABLE COMPANY.

Mr. President, Ladies and Gentlemen: — In behalf of the directors of the French Cable Company, I thank you very much for the complimentary remarks you have made concerning our telegraphic enterprise, and I also thank the company present for the manner in which they have received those remarks.

I am certain the directors take an interest — I may say a warm interest — in everything which appertains to the town of Duxbury and State of Massachusetts, insomuch that when informed that this celebration in honor of Myles Standish was about to take place, they readily testified their interest in the matter, by sending the message of congratulation which has just been read by the gentleman in the chair.

The gentlemen who sent that message are all eminent in their respective avocations in England, and it is pleasant to find that they have identified themselves with this movement to perpetuate the memory of that honored hero, Myles Standish.

Looking back in the misty space of time, I can picture in my imagination that brave old captain and his God-fearing band of followers, settling down on these once uncivilized shores, with the firm determination of worshipping God in their own way, untrammelled by fetters of political oppression to which they had been subjected in their own country, little suspecting what incalculable results would follow by this act of theirs, — results which have indelibly stamped themselves on the God-fearing character of the people of New England,— and helping to make the State of Massachusetts the first in point of piety, learning, art, and science in the United States; and I think it may be safely asserted that Myles Standish and his earnest followers were the pioneers of this wide-spread civilization.

It may, perhaps, be an interesting fact to state that the message which has just been read occupied four minutes only in transmission from London to Duxbury; this may seem incredible, but it is nevertheless a fact; and this is what is hourly, and I ought to say momentarily, accomplished by the cable which is now lying on these shores, and which could not have been placed in safer keeping than that of the descendants of the brave Myles Standish, his heroic band of followers, and the people of the State of Massachusetts.

A toast to "the Highland School Regiment, of Boston," was prefaced by some remarks complimentary to the young men who compose this company, as those who might be relied upon to keep the soldierly spirit alive, and furnish the heroes of the coming time.

The remarks were very happily responded to by Lieut. Charles H. Walker, who, in a very modest but attractive manner, said: —

"With the thanks of my Corps for the kindness with which the charming compliment has been given and received, I can only say, in the words of General James Miller, — '*We'll try, sir'!*"

A beautiful floral wreath had been presented for the table, by Mrs. Harrison Gray Otis, as also fruit and flowers by Mrs. Fletcher Webster, to which Mr. Tobey alluded in the following eloquent words: —

Almost within the lengthening shadows of this hill, in yonder cemetery of the Pilgrims, repose the remains of the great statesman of our country, whom the people of this town rejoiced not only to honor, but to recognize with affectionate regard as a friend and neighbor. We cannot forget that his memorable oration in Plymouth on the anniversary of the landing of the Pilgrim Fathers, in which he so graphically portrayed their heroic virtues and their exalted character and principles, forms one of the most valuable chapters in the history of our country. His words of burning eloquence at a later period, as he poured forth a fitting tribute to the valor and sacrifices of the patriots of the Revolution, and expressed a nation's gratitude, on the consecrated heights of Bunker Hill, are still fresh in our memory. Would that he could be here to-day, and with his inimitable power revive the historic record of the Fathers, whose memory he sacredly cherished, and which he did so much to perpetuate. With no lineal decendant to represent him here, we are glad to welcome a member of his family,* whose

* Mrs. Fletcher Webster.

interest in this occasion has found expression in a contribution of beautiful fruit and flowers, for which it gives me peculiar pleasure to present in return our cordial thanks.

I need scarcely invite attention also to the beautiful wreath which occupies so prominent a place amongst the floral decorations contributed by friends in this vicinity, whose liberality and kindness are sincerely appreciated. It is the gift of Mrs. Harrison Gray Otis, whose literary productions, not less than her patriotism, have made her name historic, and we proffer to her our most cordial thanks for this appropriate recognition of this occasion.

The venerable President Stearns, of Amherst, writes an interesting letter, in which he says: "I have spent many months, not to say years, first and last, in old Duxbury, and regard Captain's Hill as a familiar acquaintance and untiring friend. I was accustomed to dig, more than forty years ago, in the supposed ashes of Myles Standish's house, and had my search rewarded by the discovery of some old, half-burnt nails and bits of iron, which helped to contribute to the comfort of a living family once, but were chiefly valuable as humble relics of an important past, and as assisting to identify a spot which is now itself to become memorable in the history of the world. The hill itself I have visited scores of times; have seen the sun rise, dripping, as it rose from the ocean (not often), and the moon walking in her brightness across the evening firmament, and the white sails dancing on the bosom of the sea, and had the romance of old, old times come over me. The Pilgrims were much greater men and women than they knew. The more their history is studied, the more their piety, intelligence, love of liberty, political wisdom, and heroism will be admired. I have no reason to think myself a descendant of Myles Standish, that splendid "little Captain," who so often terrified the Indians, and saved our great forefathers from untimely destruction; but I have two streaks of the John Alden blood, I suppose, in my veins, and something of the same pleasant inheritance from other Mayflower progenitors; and I do not think this round globe furnishes a nobler ancestry to any classes of descendants than those same plucky, godly, far-seeing Pilgrims. Nor is there another hundred persons in the whole United States whose influence on after generations has been greater and better than theirs. As patriots and Christians, let us cherish their memories as a legacy to be guarded and improved more carefully than gold."

Dr. Oliver Wendell Holmes writes that his engagements will not permit him to be present, and adds: "The valiant little captain well deserves a memorial, and I trust that the corner-stone may soon find itself pressed down by the stately tower which promises so well in the prophetic picture you send me."

Hon. Wendell Phillips writes: "I shall not be able to accept the invitation with which you honor me, to be present at the laying of the corner-stone of the old soldier's monument. Success to it."

Other letters of regret were received from President Porter of Yale College, Gov. Jewell of Connecticut, Gov. Perham of Maine, Gov. Straw of New Hampshire, Senator Anthony of Rhode Island, Hon. Robert C. Winthrop, and others.

Miss Marcia A. Thomas, the historian of Marshfield, being unable to attend the services, from ill health, sent the following sentiment: —

"Duxborough and Green Harbor, sister townships: The dividing line defined by the Pligrim Fathers, led by Captain Myles Standish, Dec. 28, 1640. May these bounds with the 'great rock called Parting Rock,' whence they commenced their survey, ever remain unchanged!"

Lieutenant-General Sheridan writes from Chicago that "it would afford him great pleasure to be one of your number on the occasion, but the pressure of public duties renders it impossible for me to promise to attend."

General Sherman writes: "I have been away so much that I must ask you to excuse me. After an absence of ten months in Europe, you can easily see that I have both private and public matters encugh to absorb all my time till Christmas."

Vice-President Colfax says: "I regret that your exercises, to which you have so kindly invited me, are to occur on the day before the Indiana State election, as that fact renders my presence with you impossible."

Henry W. Longfellow sends his "thanks and regrets," but owing to other engagements will not be able to attend.

Although regretting the absence of Gen. William T. Sherman, his friends received, with gratitude, the following telegram: —

"WASHINGTON, D. C., Oct. 7, 1872.

STEPHEN M. ALLEN, *Corresponding Secretary Standish Monument Association, South Duxbury, Mass.*: —

May the monument you inaugurate this day to the first captain of New England, stand forever as a beacon to guide the descendants of the Pilgrims in the path of courage and virtue that made Myles Standish a man among men, a hero among heroes.

W. T. SHERMAN, *General.*"

Gen. John A. Dix, having telegraphed the following message, its reading was greeted with applause: —

"NEW YORK, Oct. 7th, 1872.

STEPHEN M. ALLEN, *Secretary Myles Standish Association, Duxbury*: —

All honor to the great New-England captain, and the New-England virtues which he illustrated. I send from a distance what I cannot offer in person, — the tribute of my sincere respects.

JOHN A. DIX."

This telegram, from General Sheridan, was received too late for reading at the dinner table : —

"CHICAGO, ILL., Oct. 7, 1872.

General Horace Binney Sargent : — Allow me to offer my congratulations upon the commencement of the monument erected to the first commissioned military officer of the colonies in America. Your work to-day proves that his works were worthy, for his fame stands the test of time.

P. H. SHERIDAN, *Lieut-Gen. U. S. A.*"

A vote was passed complimentary to the press and reporters, with thanks for their valuable assistance, as also for the Old Colony Railroad Company, for their valuable contribution to the celebration.

The proceedings closed with the reading of congratulatory despatches from distinguished persons.

Rev. A. Parke Burgess briefly responded for the clergy of Duxbury, and Mr. Nathaniel Adams made a brief statement relative to the construction of the monument, which is to cost about $30,000. This closed the exercises in the tent, and the company separated.

The battalion never appeared to better advantage than it did yesterday, both in point of numbers and excellent military bearing, and its members will long cherish with feelings of pleasure the fall field-day of 1872, and their trip to Duxbury. The revenue cutter Mahoning steamed up to the wharf just as the ceremony at the corner-stone was completed, and fired a national salute in honor of the occasion.

Special trains left immediately after the proceedings had closed. The Artillery left Duxbury shortly after six o'clock, and were landed in Boston about eight o'clock, when they were marched direct to their armory and there dismissed. Too much praise cannot be accorded to Superintendent Kendrick of the Old Colony Railroad for the excellent arrangements made for the conveyance of the visitors, and to the committee of arrangements on behalf of the Ancients, of which Colonel John L. Stevenson was chairman, for the care taken of that and other organizations.

In the compilation of the proceedings at the celebration, the Corresponding Secretary has been assisted very much by liberal quotations from the Boston press, which have ever rendered good service to the Association. The original papers and notes of the occasion, together with some eight hundred manuscript letters from distinguished men of the country, who sympathized deeply with the Association, having been consumed by the late fire, it has been difficult to recollect or reproduce a record of the proceedings on Captain's Hill which could compare favorably with the one first made; and without the aid of the notes of the press it would have been quite impossible.

The letters above, overflowing as they were with sympathy and admiration for the cause, would have made a fine volume to the honor of the Pilgrim Captain, and of which his descendants and all who honor his name, would have felt justly proud. Such honor has seldom been paid to a citizen of any period in the history of the United States. And it is a subject of congratulation that the enterprise has succeeded so well.

The mason work went on under the personal direction of Edwin Adams, Esq., till the frost prevented further progress for the winter, and one month's work in the spring will finish the octagon base of the monument, which is by far the most difficult and expensive part of the structure. The stones for the whole work are all contracted for, and are nearly all on the ground ready for laying, and at the earliest moment, when the proper workmen can be spared from the great Boston ruin, the whole will be speedily finished.

Many of the stones for the base of the edifice were very massive, weighing between four and five tons, but they were transported to the top of the hill without difficulty by six yoke of large oxen, and by the aid of immense derricks, were placed in position.

The general government has named the channel running to the foot of Captain's Hill "Myles Channel," in honor of the Pilgrim commander, and they have also appropriated $20,000 for putting it in good condition for navigation, and as a harbor of refuge in case of storms. This shows an appreciation of Captain Standish, and the memorial that is being erected to his memory, which also serves an important interest in the coast survey and navigation.

And thus, after a flight of two hundred and fifty years, a grate ful people have demonstrated their appreciation of one of the noblest and bravest of men. This appreciation is not confined to the Old Colony, the State of Massachusetts, or New England. It has the Nation's seal, and bears the type of a Nation's glory.

An individual interest before unheard of on such a subject, has poured in, and two thousand letters, from almost every State and hamlet in the Union, contribute an expression of the strongest feeling, indorsing the worth of him for whom this structure has been commenced. This sentiment has not been entirely confined to our own country. Europe has remembered through the turn of centuries, a man that has reflected so much glory upon his native land from his untiring labors and devotion, his patriotic valor and worth, in founding a new and distant one, which already fills an important place in the galaxy of nations.

www.ingramcontent.com/pod-product-compliance
Lightning Source LLC
LaVergne TN
LVHW021409110826
845150LV00007B/1845